Number 130
Summer 2011

New Directions for Evaluation

Sandra Mathison
Editor-in-Chief

Advancing Validity in Outcome Evaluation: Theory and Practice

Huey T. Chen
Stewart I. Donaldson
Melvin M. Mark
Editors

ADVANCING VALIDITY IN OUTCOME EVALUATION: THEORY AND PRACTICE
Huey T. Chen, Stewart I. Donaldson, Melvin M. Mark (eds.)
New Directions for Evaluation, no. 130
Sandra Mathison, Editor-in-Chief

Microfilm copies of issues and articles are available in 16mm and 35mm, as well as microfiche in 105mm, through University Microfilms Inc., 300 North Zeeb Road, Ann Arbor, MI 48106-1346.

New Directions for Evaluation is indexed in Cambridge Scientific Abstracts (CSA/CIG), Contents Pages in Education (T & F), Higher Education Abstracts (Claremont Graduate University), Social Services Abstracts (CSA/CIG), Sociological Abstracts (CSA/CIG), and Worldwide Political Sciences Abstracts (CSA/CIG).

NEW DIRECTIONS FOR EVALUATION (ISSN 1097-6736, electronic ISSN 1534-875X) is part of The Jossey-Bass Education Series and is published quarterly by Wiley Subscription Services, Inc., A Wiley Company, at Jossey-Bass, 989 Market Street, San Francisco, CA 94103-1741.

SUBSCRIPTIONS cost $89 for U.S./Canada/Mexico; $113 international. For institutions, agencies, and libraries, $271 U.S.; $311 Canada/Mexico; $345 international. Prices subject to change.

EDITORIAL CORRESPONDENCE should be addressed to the Editor-in-Chief, Sandra Mathison, University of British Columbia, 2125 Main Mall, Vancouver, BC V6T 1Z4, Canada.

www.josseybass.com

Editorial Policy and Procedures

New Directions for Evaluation, a quarterly sourcebook, is an official publication of the American Evaluation Association. The journal publishes empirical, methodological, and theoretical works on all aspects of evaluation. A reflective approach to evaluation is an essential strand to be woven through every issue. The editors encourage issues that have one of three foci: (1) craft issues that present approaches, methods, or techniques that can be applied in evaluation practice, such as the use of templates, case studies, or survey research; (2) professional issues that present topics of import for the field of evaluation, such as utilization of evaluation or locus of evaluation capacity; (3) societal issues that draw out the implications of intellectual, social, or cultural developments for the field of evaluation, such as the women's movement, communitarianism, or multiculturalism. A wide range of substantive domains is appropriate for *New Directions for Evaluation;* however, the domains must be of interest to a large audience within the field of evaluation. We encourage a diversity of perspectives and experiences within each issue, as well as creative bridges between evaluation and other sectors of our collective lives.

The editors do not consider or publish unsolicited single manuscripts. Each issue of the journal is devoted to a single topic, with contributions solicited, organized, reviewed, and edited by a guest editor. Issues may take any of several forms, such as a series of related chapters, a debate, or a long article followed by brief critical commentaries. In all cases, the proposals must follow a specific format, which can be obtained from the editor-in-chief. These proposals are sent to members of the editorial board and to relevant substantive experts for peer review. The process may result in acceptance, a recommendation to revise and resubmit, or rejection. However, the editors are committed to working constructively with potential guest editors to help them develop acceptable proposals.

Sandra Mathison, Editor-in-Chief
University of British Columbia
2125 Main Mall
Vancouver, BC V6T 1Z4
CANADA
e-mail: nde@eval.org

CONTENTS

EDITORS' NOTES

D ecades ago, Suchman (1967) encouraged evaluators to apply Campbell and Stanley's (Campbell & Stanley, 1963) writings on experiments, quasi-experiments, and validity to evaluation. Since that time, the Campbellian validity typology, as presented in Campbell and Stanley (1963), Cook and Campbell (1979), and Shadish, Cook, and Campbell (2002), has been prominent in much of the theory and practice of outcome evaluation. Despite its influence, the Campbellian validity typology and its associated methods have been criticized, sometimes generating heated debates on the typology's strengths and weaknesses for evaluation. For some readers such debates might form part of this issue's subtext; for others the issue should still be of interest—even to evaluators new to the field and unfamiliar with such debates. Validity frameworks are important. They can inform thinking about evaluation, guide evaluation practice, and facilitate future development of evaluation theory and methods.

This issue had its origins in a panel at the 2008 conference of the American Evaluation Association. Led by Huey T. Chen, the session focused on theory and practice as related to external validity in evaluation. The session was motivated in part by the sense that new directions, and perhaps increased attention to some old directions, are needed to reach meaningful conclusions about evaluation generalizability. But session presenters addressed issues related to validity forms beyond external validity. In addition, as planning shifted from the conference session to this issue, newly added contributors planned to address issues other than external validity. As a result, after considering alternative framings, the issue has evolved to its theme, that is, validity in the context of outcome evaluation.

The primary focus of most of the chapters is not on Campbell and colleagues' validity typology per se, but rather on its application in the context of outcome evaluation. According to the Program Evaluation Standards (Joint Committee on Standards for Educational Evaluation, 1994), four attributes are essential for evaluation practice: utility, feasibility, propriety, and accuracy. The Campbellian typology offers clear strengths in addressing accuracy. However, it is less suited to address issues of utility, propriety, and feasibility. Perhaps a worthwhile direction for developing a comprehensive validity perspective for evaluation is to build on the Campbellian typology in ways that will better address issues related to all four attributes. This issue of *New Directions for Evaluation* is organized and developed under this spirit.

Disclaimer: The findings and conclusions of this article are those of the authors and do not necessarily represent the official position of the Centers for Disease Control and Prevention (CDC).

NEW DIRECTIONS FOR EVALUATION, no. 130, Summer 2011 © Wiley Periodicals, Inc., and the American Evaluation Association. Published online in Wiley Online Library (wileyonlinelibrary.com) • DOI: 10.1002/ev.360

1

In general, we take the stance that we can further advance validity in outcome evaluation by revising or expanding the Campbellian typology. Chapter authors present multiple views on how to build on the Campbellian typology's contribution and suggest alternative validity frameworks or models to serve program evaluation better. We hope that these new perspectives will advance theory and practice regarding validity in evaluation as well as improve the quality and usefulness of outcome evaluations.

Chapter authors propose the following strategies in developing a new perspective of validity typology for advancing validity in program evaluation.

Enhance External Validity

John Gargani and Stewart I. Donaldson, then Melvin M. Mark, focus on external validity. Gargani and Donaldson discuss limits of the Campbellian tradition regarding external validity. They argue that the external validity of an evaluation could be enhanced by better addressing issues about what works for whom, where, why, and when. Mark reviews several alternative framings of generalizability issues. With the use of these alternatives, he provides potentially fruitful directions for external validity enhancement.

Enhance Precision by Reclassifying the Campbellian Typology

The chapters by Charles S. Reichardt and George Julnes offer conceptual revisions of the Campbellian typology. Reichardt offers what he sees as flaws in the four types of validity in Shadish et al. (2002). He also offers his version of a typology, which includes four criteria: validity, precision, generalizability, and completeness. Julnes proposes a validity framework with three dimensions—representation (construct validity), causal inference (internal and external validity), and valuation. He argues for the conceptual and pragmatic merits of this framework.

Expand the Scope of the Typology

Ernest R. House discusses the Campbellian typology's limitations in dealing with ethical challenges with which evaluation is increasingly faced. He notes an alarming phenomenon, visible in medical evaluations but increasingly worrisome in other areas of evaluation practice, whereby evaluation results become biased because of researchers' intentional and unintentional manipulation. House discusses strategies for dealing with this ethical problem, including how these ethics-related problems might be incorporated within the Campbellian validity tradition.

Jennifer C. Greene is one of the few contributors to this issue who is not affiliated with the Campbellian tradition. She provides a naturalistic viewpoint in examining limits of the Campbellian typology. She discusses different validity concepts and offers strategies for strengthening validity that are not primarily associated with the Campbellian tradition. At the same time, her comments are congenial to advances within the framework provided by Campbell and colleagues. Huey T. Chen and Paul Garbe argue that outcome evaluation should address system-integration issues that go beyond the scope of goal attainment. The Campbellian typology's strength is goal-attainment assessment. To address both goal-attainment and system-integration issues, these authors propose a validity model with three categories: viable, effectual, and transferable. With this expanded typology, they propose a bottom-up approach with the use of quantitative and qualitative methods to strengthen validity in an evaluation.

William R. Shadish, a collaborator of Campbell's who played a key role in expanding the Campbellian typology (Shadish et al., 2002), offers his perspective on the contributions of this issue. Other chapters in the issue discuss various aspects of the Campbellian typology, with the authors representing varying degrees of closeness or distance to the tradition. Shadish speaks as an involved and interested representative of this tradition, which he upholds with vigor, thus providing balance to the perspectives in the issue. Shadish clarifies and defends the work of Campbell and his colleagues, offers themes related to the issue topic, and comments on the rest of the chapters.

Shadish takes exception with many of the arguments in the other chapters, countering our view that the typology must be revised or expanded to serve program evaluation better. Our hope is that the interplay among the ideas in all of the chapters will provide readers with multiple viewpoints as well as stimulate future development in this important area. Don Campbell advocated a "disputatious community of scholars" to create self-correcting processes. He appended critiques of his papers by others to his own reprints. In this spirit, we include Shadish's comments and hope this will contribute to evaluators' thinking and practice regarding validity and outcome evaluation.

References

Campbell, D. T., & Stanley, J. C. (1963). Experimental and quasi-experimental designs for research on teaching. In N. L. Gage (Ed.), *Handbook of research on teaching* (pp. 171–246). Chicago, IL: Rand McNally. Also published as Campbell, D. T., & Stanley, J. C. (1966). *Experimental and quasi-experimental designs for research.* Chicago, IL: Rand McNally. Since reprinted as Campbell, D. T., & Stanley, J. (1963). *Experimental and quasi-experimental designs for research.* Boston, MA: Houghton-Mifflin/Wadsworth.

Cook, T. D., & Campbell, D. T. (1979). *Quasi-experimentation: Design and analysis issues for field settings.* Chicago, IL: Rand McNally.

Joint Committee on Standards for Educational Evaluation. (1994). *The program evaluation standards* (2nd ed.). Thousand Oaks, CA: Sage.

Shadish, W. R., Cook, T. D., & Campbell, D. T. (2002). *Experimental and quasi-experimental designs for generalized causal inference.* Boston, MA: Houghton Mifflin.
Suchman, E. A. (1967). *Evaluation research.* New York, NY: Russell Sage Foundation.

Huey T. Chen
Stewart I. Donaldson
Melvin M. Mark
Editors

HUEY T. CHEN *is a senior evaluation scientist of the Air Pollution and Respiratory Health Branch at the Centers for Disease Control and Prevention (CDC).*

STEWART I. DONALDSON *is dean and professor of psychology at the Claremont Graduate University.*

MELVIN M. MARK *is professor and head of psychology at Penn State University.*

NEW DIRECTIONS FOR EVALUATION • DOI: 10.1002/ev

Chen, H. T., Donaldson, S. I., & Mark, M. M. (2011). Validity frameworks for outcome evaluation. In H. T. Chen, S. I. Donaldson, & M. M. Mark (Eds.), *Advancing validity in outcome evaluation: Theory and practice. New Directions for Evaluation, 130,* 5–16.

1

Validity Frameworks for Outcome Evaluation

Huey T. Chen, Stewart I. Donaldson, Melvin M. Mark

Abstract

*This chapter discusses the concept of validity as it applies to outcome evalua-
tion. We address the historical adoption and contributions of the Campbellian
typology to evaluation. We also discuss related criticisms and controversies and
address future directions.* © Wiley Periodicals, Inc., and the American Eval
uation Association.

How does an evaluator conclude that a program works? How skeptically should a potential evaluation consumer view a summary statement such as "The Web-based supplementary instruction program
increased mathematics performance by the equivalent of 3 months of regular instruction"? And how skeptically should that same evaluation consumer view the conclusion that similar effects would occur at her school
district? From one perspective at least, the concept of validity lies at the core
of all such questions.

Disclaimer: The findings and conclusions of this article are those of the authors and do
not necessarily represent the official position of the Centers for Disease Control and Prevention (CDC).

New Directions for Evaluation, no. 130, Summer 2011   © Wiley Periodicals, Inc., and the American Evaluation
Association.   Published online in Wiley Online Library (wileyonlinelibrary.com) • DOI: 10.1002/ev.361

Campbellian Validity Typology

In discussing the Campbellian validity typology, it may be important to start with what the typology is not. The term *validity* has been broadly applied, with test validity perhaps the most common usage (Lissitz, 2009; Messick, 1989). Psychometricians, education measurement specialists, and practitioners in areas ranging from personnel selection to compensatory education care mightily about whether, for example, a 25-item multiple-choice test is valid. In a test-validity context, alternative conceptualizations of validity exist (Lissitz, 2009). The classic view is that test validity refers to the extent to which a test measures what it is supposed to measure. A more recent conceptualization of test validity argues that validity refers to the extent to which any interpretations and actions based on the test are justified.

The focus of this chapter is not on test validity, but rather on the forms of validity that occur in the Campbellian typology and in outcome evaluation. Accordingly, this issue focuses on validity issues that arise when evaluators investigate the relationship between an intervention (e.g., a health promotion or social service program) and the potential outcomes of interest (e.g., reduced childhood obesity or increased employment). Program evaluation commonly requires convincing and defensible evidence about the outcomes of an intervention. In this regard, the Campbellian validity typology has attracted evaluators' attention. It provides a conceptual framework for thinking about evaluation design and certain kinds of challenges, and it highlights potential strengths and weaknesses of methods that evaluators might use to address validity issues in an outcome evaluation.

As with this entire issue, this introductory chapter focuses on validity in the context of what are varyingly referred to as *outcome* or *impact evaluations*. In this introductory chapter, we provide an overview of the Campbellian validity typology. This overview is designed to enhance the ability to read and benefit from the rest of this issue, especially for those less familiar with the Campbellian framework. Readers already familiar with the validity framework of Campbell and his colleagues should also find points of interest.

Content of the Campbellian Validity Framework

We suggest that the Campbellian validity typology contains three general content areas: the nature of validity, the types of validity in the context of estimating treatment effects (and threats to each type of validity), and the principles or procedures for prioritization across validity types. Methods for addressing validity issues could also be viewed as a fourth content area of the validity typology, but alternatively can be seen as another, related component in a broader theory of validity and methods. We briefly and selectively address each of these areas. For a fuller discussion of the validity concept and methods, we encourage readers to consult the original sources.

Nature of Validity

Whether by evaluators or others, secondary discussions of Campbell's validity typology, including the variants associated with co-authors Stanley, Cook, and Shadish and Cook, focus largely on the types of validity in the typology (and on the threats to each type of validity). Although more nuanced distinctions are available, it appears that validity definitions can take several different approaches, including:

1. Validity as the accuracy of an inference. For example, if an evaluation concludes that Early Head Start substantially increases school readiness, does that conclusion correspond to the actual (but not directly known) state of the world?
2. Validity as property of method/research design. For example, if a randomized experiment is taken as having excellent internal validity, then any well-conducted experimental evaluation is thought to have strong internal validity.

Campbell and Stanley open their discussion by saying that "In this chapter we shall examine the validity of sixteen experimental designs against twelve common threats to valid inference" (Campbell & Stanley, 1963, p. 1). Although not explicitly stated, it appears that some readers have taken such language as implying that validity is a property of method, specifically of a quasi-experimental or experimental design. By this interpretation, for instance, a one-group, pretest–posttest design is taken as weak with respect to internal validity because threats including maturation, history, and testing are all plausible in general. Interpreting validity as a design property does not comport well with the broader body of Campbell's writing, but appears common in many descriptions written by others about the validity framework of Campbell and colleagues.

Generally speaking, Cook and Campbell took a validity-as-accuracy perspective. They stated that "We shall use the concepts validity and invalidity to refer to the best available approximation to the truth or falsity of propositions" (Cook and Campbell, 1979, p. 39). And they indicated that factors other than design are important in tentatively establishing validity claims (e.g., qualitative investigation may clarify whether history threats occurred in a quasi-experiment). Shadish, Cook, and Campbell (2002, p. 33) reported they "use the term *validity* to refer to the approximate truth of an inference," and they further indicated that their concept of validity is informed by both correspondence and coherence conceptions of truth, as well as pragmatism (pp. 35–37). This more recent definition of validity seems congruent with Campbell's work in general, including his emphasis on the fallibility of all knowledge claims, concepts such as plausible alternative explanations and validity threats, and the logic of ruling out plausible alternative interpretations. In contrast, the validity-as-property-of method notion, while implicit in some writing about Campbell, does not fit well with his broader body of work (see the Shadish, Cook, & Leviton, 1991, detailed summary of Campbell's writing).

Types of Validity

To date, the Campbellian typology has appeared in three major versions. Campbell and Stanley (1963) offered the initial version. They proposed a distinction between internal validity and external validity. They defined internal validity in terms of whether ". . . in fact the experimental treatments make a difference in this specific experimental instance?" Campbell and Stanley further specified that external validity asks the question of generalizability: "To what populations, settings, treatment variables, and measurement variables can this effect be generalized?"

Cook and Campbell (1979) expanded on the Campbell and Stanley listing of validity types, identifying four types rather than two. Cook and Campbell (1979) subdivided internal validity into two types: statistical conclusion validity and internal validity. The former involves validity related to the question of what "conclusions about covariation are made on the basis of statistical evidence." Internal validity involves the accuracy of the conclusion about whether there is a causal relationship between the treatment and the outcome(s), given the particular setting and participants observed and the particular methods employed. Similarly, Cook and Campbell also subdivided Campbell and Stanley's external validity into two categories: construct validity and external validity. Construct validity involves the validity of conclusions about "what are the particular cause and effect constructs involved in the relationship?" External validity involves the question of "how generalizable is the causal relationship to and across persons, setting, and times?"

Shadish et al. (2002) used the same four validity types proposed by Cook and Campbell (1979). In the more recent version, the definitions of statistical conclusion and internal validity remain the same, whereas the definitions of construct and external validity are slightly modified. To Shadish et al. (2002), construct validity refers to the "validity of inference about the higher order constructs that represent sampling particulars." By contrast, external validity refers to "whether the causal relationship holds over variation in persons, settings, treatments, and measurement variables." That is, Cook and Campbell linked construct validity to treatment and outcomes, and external validity to persons and settings; in contrast, Shadish et al. (2002) extended both validities to each of the four facets of a study they highlight: persons, treatments, outcomes, and settings.

The validity concepts emanating from the evolving validity typology of Campbell and his associates have established a strong presence in the evaluation literature. The initial distinction between internal and external validity, popularized by Campbell and Stanley (1963), is widely used today. In this issue, as in the rest of the literature, authors differ in terms of which version they emphasize. The Reichardt (this issue), Julnes (this issue), and Mark (this issue) chapters focus on the Cook and Campbell (1979) and Shadish et al. (2002) versions, whereas the rest of the chapters primarily refer to the Campbell and Stanley version.

Principles of Prioritization

In addition to specifying (two or four) validity types, the Campbellian typology offers principles for prioritizing various validity types. Campbell and Stanley (1963) pointed out the frequent trade-offs between internal and external validity. That is, an increase in one may come only with a reduction of the other. For example, a limited set of sites may allow random assignment to condition (or the use of other design features that facilitate internal validity), and these sites may be unusual in ways that hinder generalization results to other sites.

For Campbell and Stanley (1963), the first priority is internal validity. For them, internal validity is the minimum requirement for any cause-probing study, without which research results are difficult to interpret. An oft-quoted statement of theirs is that "internal validity is the sine qua non." Of course, although placing a priority on internal validity, Campbell and Stanley described both internal and external validity as important. After all, Campbell developed and helped to popularize the external validity concept, at least in part so that concerns about generalization would not be ignored.

Cook and Campbell (1979) offer a more nuanced discussion, highlighting, for example, that the Campbell and Stanley priority to internal validity assumes that a study's purpose was to investigate whether a treatment affected an outcome. In the context of evaluation, then, Campbell and Stanley's prioritization of internal validity would not apply to evaluations that have some other focus. Thus, claims about so-called gold-standard methods, without caveats about evaluation purpose, seem inconsistent with a careful reading of Campbell's work.

More recently, Shadish et al. (2002, p. 98) advanced an even more nuanced view than Cook and Campbell about priorities across validity types. For example, they state that "internal validity is not the sine qua non of all research" and that it "has a special (but not inviolate) place in cause-probing research, especially in experimental research." They also advocated for *programs of research* in which studies varied in their relative prioritization of different validity types, with each validity type having "its turn in the spotlight" across studies (p. 102).

Methods for Enhancing Validity

Another important validity-related contribution made by Campbell and his associates was their specification of various experimental and quasi-experimental designs for enhancing a study's internal validity. They systematically illustrated how in general each design does or does not rule out threats to internal validity. Internal validity threats are categories of generic alternative explanations, such as history or maturation, which could alternatively account for what might appear to be an effect of the program on the outcome of interest. According to Campbell and his associates, randomized experiments are generally preferable for estimating a treatment effect because they typically can rule out most threats to internal validity (where "rule out" is a term commonly used for rendering a threat implausible). In spite of this preference, Campbell and colleagues cautioned that experimental methods should be applied thoughtfully. For example, an automatic priority for randomized controlled trials (RCTs) would likely ignore caveats from the Campbellian tradition, such as "Premature experimental work is a common research sin" (Shadish et al., 2002, p. 99). Quasi-experimental methods are generally a second-best choice, with a wide range across quasi-experimental designs in terms of how well they typically rule out the majority of threats to internal validity. Again, however, as Shadish et al. especially make clear, a one-to-one correspondence between research design and validity should not be assumed. Additional evidence can help strengthen or refute validity claims.

Although external validity was originally viewed as a lower priority than internal validity, Campbell and his associates made noteworthy contributions to our understanding of external validity. Of course, developing and popularizing the concept itself were major accomplishments. Moreover, Campbell and colleagues increasingly offered methods and principles for enhancing external validity. Cook and Campbell (1979) discussed alternative methods for sampling, for example, including purposive sampling of different kinds of cases (to see if findings held across the differences in question) or sampling "modal instances," cases most like those to which generalization is desired. Shadish et al. (2002) also offered principles for enhancing external validity. They discussed enhancing external validity by surface similarity, ruling out irrelevancies, making discriminations, interpolation, and causal explanation. Despite these contributions, much of the conversation about enhancing external validity is at a different level conceptually from that of internal validity. And contributors to the evaluation literature have done much less than might be desired in terms of applying, revising, and adding to the methods and principles for enhancing external validity.

The Campbellian Validity Typology and Program Evaluation

Although some may disagree, we believe that comprehensive program evaluation requires credible evidence of an intervention's effectuality. And the Campbellian validity typology provides valuable concepts and suggests methods for addressing this evaluation need. Not surprisingly, then, the Campbellian typology has been influential in program evaluation, including coverage in major evaluation textbooks.

The Campbellian typology has also gained additional momentum from the current evidence-based interventions movement, which started in medicine and has spread to the public and to many social and behavioral disciplines under a general label of evidence-based interventions (Donaldson, Christie, & Mark, 2008). Much of the evidence-based intervention movement echoes early arguments made by Campbell and Stanley about the priority on internal validity and the strengths of RCTs for producing credible evidence. An increasing number of funding agencies have become interested in promoting evidence-based interventions and scientific evaluation (Huffman & Lawrenz, 2006).

Critiques of Campbellian Typology

In spite of its popularity and its influence, the Campbellian typology has been criticized, sometimes sharply, by some evaluators. Key criticisms can be classified as follows.

Criticism 1. Internal Validity Should Not Be the Top Priority

Cronbach (1982, p. 137) strongly disagreed with the idea that priority should be given to internal validity. He claimed that internal validity is "trivial, past-tense, and local." Instead, he argued external validity should have priority, because it is future oriented and addresses issues more interesting to decision makers. Cronbach viewed a profitable evaluation as one that could draw stakeholders' attention to relevant factors and influence their decisions. In this view, evaluations need to allow extrapolation from the evaluation's specific populations, treatments, measures, and settings, to other instances of each of these that are of interest to decision makers. For instance, an evaluation might include specific sites and clients, but a decision maker might be interested in judgments about whether to implement the program at another location with the kinds of prospective clients present there.

One of the consequences of giving priority to internal validity has been relative neglect of external validity. Evaluators, especially in health promotion, increasingly recognize that the neglect of external validity has resulted in delivery information that is not sufficiently relevant to stakeholders, which in turn has contributed to a huge gap between academic and practical communities (Chen, 2005; Green & Glasgow, 2006; Wandersman et al., 2008). Exceptions exist, such as the use of meta-analysis to examine how program effects vary across client subgroups and settings, and evaluations that examine how variations in program characteristics are associated with different outcomes. Despite such exceptions, a growing movement encourages more emphasis on external validity in evaluation.

Criticism 2. RCTs Are Not the Best Method for Obtaining Credible Evidence About the Kinds of Questions Evaluators Should Address

Writings from the Campbellian tradition are cited by advocates of the wide use of RCTs, despite caveats in that tradition (Shadish et al., 2002). The evaluation community nonetheless remains deeply divided. Ongoing and at times heated debates continue on the relative merits of RCTs (Donaldson et al., 2008). Many evaluators, often influenced by Campbell, view RCTs as the best method for providing rigorous evidence about the efficacy of an intervention. They cite examples of false claims about intervention effectuality from evaluations using other methods. Counterarguments are easy to find, often drawing on one or more of the following: (a) methodological criticisms, such as Scriven's (2008) contention that double blinding (i.e., neither participants nor researchers know which conditions a participant is in) is essential for quality RCTs, but, because this cannot done in typical program evaluations, RCTs are susceptible to Hawthorne and related expectancy effects; (b) practical considerations, such as claims that RCTs are difficult to implement successfully in the field, especially within decision timelines; and (c) contextual considerations, such as Greene's (2008) joining Cronbach (1982) in criticizing narrowly defined evaluations that ignore the power of contextual influences on an intervention.

Criticism 3. Persuasion, Interpretation, and the Subjective Nature of Conclusions Should Be Emphasized, Rather Than Validity

Another general criticism of the Campbellian validity typology involves a fundamental question of the notion of validity. These critics say that this view of validity is anchored in positivist and postpositivist thought. Such critics instead embrace the phenomenological paradigm's viewpoint, while also promoting naturalistic inquiry in an effort to understand human experience in natural settings more inductively and holistically. As a result, advocates of such alternatives would propose different criteria for judging trustworthiness of an inquiry (Maxwell, 1992). For example, Guba and Lincoln (1989) proposed four criteria for judging an inquiry's soundness: *Credibility* refers to whether research results are believable from the perspective of the research participants. *Transferability* refers to whether the research results can be transferred to other contexts or settings. *Dependability* refers to demonstrating that the findings are consistent and could be repeated with the same or similar respondents in the same or similar situations. *Confirmability* refers to a degree to which the inquiry results are shaped by the respondents and not by researcher biases.

In this issue of *New Directions for Evaluation*, this tradition is represented primarily in Greene's chapter.

Relationship Between the Campbellian Typology and Program Evaluation

The Campbellian typology has provided useful guidance for outcome evaluation, but has also helped fuel controversies and criticisms that may confuse practicing evaluators. To improve understanding of validity issues, program evaluation must at least put the conflicting views in perspective and might even attempt to reconcile their differences. The first step in such efforts may be to recognize the difference in the intended research scope of the Campbellian typology and the application of the Campbellian typology for serving evaluation purposes.

On the one hand, Campbell and Stanley (1963) clearly indicated that their typology was developed for experimental and near-experimental research intended to study the effects of interventions for teaching and learning from the beginning. Similarly, subsequent work (Cook & Campbell, 1979; Shadish et al., 2002) also focuses on studies intended to assess the effects of treatments, emphasizing social and behavioral research in field settings. In fact, all three books hardly mention the word "evaluation." On the other hand, despite its intended application for general cause-probing (specifically, effect estimating) studies in field research, the Campbellian typology has been intensively applied in the arena of outcome evaluation. Indeed, the appropriation of Campbell's thinking into evaluation by Suchman led to his becoming an "accidental evaluator" (Shadish & Luellen, 2004). The resulting influence has been considerable, with Campbell regarded as a seminal figure in program evaluation (Alkin, 2004; Shadish et al., 1991).

In spite of its intensive application in evaluation, it appears that Campbell and his associates (Campbell & Stanley, 1963; Cook & Campbell, 1979; Shadish et al., 2002) have not clearly and directly stated whether the Campbellian typology as it stands is appropriate or sufficient for use in program evaluation, at least in the books that present the evolving typology. Again, all three of these books hardly mention the word *evaluation*. Other writings by key partners in the Campbellian tradition do clearly suggest a broader view of evaluation for which the Campbellian validity typology would not suffice (e.g., Shadish et al., 1991). The lack of shared agreement about the intended role of the typology in evaluation might be an obstacle preventing proponents and opponents of the typology from engaging in constructive debates on validity issues in the evaluation community. Differing interpretations of the adequacy of the Campbellian typology for evaluation may be an obstacle. It may lead some proponents to focus too narrowly on a limited set of methods, and to overstate the relative frequency of outcome evaluation. It may also keep proponents and opponents of the typology from engaging in constructive debate. For example, opponents can criticize the typology based upon its inadequacy for evaluation as a whole, whereas proponents can make counterarguments based upon its broad value for causal research—with each side taking solace in their argument, even though they are talking about different things.

To clarify this issue, Chen (2010) pointed out that the Campbellian typology is developed for research rather than outcome evaluation and discussed its strengths and limitations from this standpoint. In essence, there may be costs of treating the Campbellian validity typology and related work as a complete theory of evaluation (which, again, it was not designed to be). Although some evaluations use experimental or quasi-experimental designs to determine a program's outcomes, many use other types of designs and approaches to address a wide range of questions about a program (Donaldson, 2007).

Toward a New Perspective of a Comprehensive Validity Typology for Program Evaluation

We believe without question that the Campbellian validity typology has made an important contribution to program evaluation. However, the typology was not developed for program evaluation, so not surprisingly we also believe there are limits to how far it can help to advance evaluation. The controversies and heated debates related to the typology suggest that its contribution to evaluation may have reached a limit at the current stage of program evaluation, at least in the absence of further elaboration, expansion, or revision. It is up to evaluators to develop a more comprehensive perspective for further advancing validity in outcome evaluation. There are three potential profitable directions for this advancement.

One way of advancing the relationship between the Campbellian validity typology and program evaluation is to specify the other forms and purposes of evaluation that do not fit well with the typology's focus on assessing the effects of a given treatment. This may not seem necessary, given the long-standing attention to formative evaluation, needs assessment, stakeholder procedures for uncovering program theories and valued outcomes, and the like. However, given the background of debates about RCTs as a gold standard, it is worth restating that even early advocates of random assignment studies and the priority of internal validity do not argue for these as comprehensive preferences for the entire array of evaluation practice. Likewise, it is worth highlighting that the Campbellian typology and related methods are of limited if any relevance to the evaluation tasks that do not involve estimating the effects of a program or other evaluand.

A second way to improve the contribution between the Campbellian framework and program evaluation is to highlight aspects of the work of Campbell and colleagues that have not received adequate attention in evaluation. For example, Mark (this issue) notes several techniques and concepts related to external validity from the Campbellian tradition. He argues that increased attention to these, as well as to stakeholder-based procedures, could improve understanding about generalizability and its bounds in evaluation.

However, highlighting existing aspects of the existing Campbellian framework can only go so far. Thus, a third way to clarify the relationship between the Campbellian framework and program evaluation, taken by almost all of the contributors to the present issue (Number 130) of *New Directions for Evaluation*, is to examine the typology's adequacy for outcome evaluation, the area of evaluation to which it has typically been applied. In general, contributors to this issue recognize the major contributions made by Campbell and his colleagues in their work on validity. However, they also suggest limits, as well as possible improvements in the form of elaborations and revisions for evaluation applications. The suggested revisions largely arise from perceived problems of fit between the Campbell validity typology and the needs of outcome evaluation, including the potential use of such evaluations in policy and practice settings. Our hope is that, by addressing ways of expanding or revising the Campbellian framework, the pieces in this issue will enhance thought and practice related to the validity of outcome evaluation.

References

Alkin, M. C. (Ed.). (2004). *Evaluation roots: Tracing theorists' views and influences.* Thousand Oaks, CA: Sage.

Campbell, D. T., & Stanley, J. C. (1963). Experimental and quasi-experimental designs for research on teaching. In N. L. Gage (Ed.), *Handbook of research on teaching* (pp. 171–246). Chicago, IL: Rand McNally. Also published as Campbell, D. T., & Stanley, J. C. (1966). *Experimental and quasi-experimental designs for research.* Chicago, IL: Rand McNally. Since reprinted as Campbell, D. T., & Stanley, J. (1963). *Experimental and quasi-experimental designs for research.* Boston, MA: Houghton-Mifflin/Wadsworth.

Chen, H. T. (2005). *Practical program evaluation: Assessing and improving planning, implementation, and effectiveness.* Thousand Oaks, CA: Sage.

Chen, H. T. (2010). The bottom-up approach to integrative validity: A new perspective for program evaluation. *Evaluation and Program Planning, 33*(3), 205–214.

Cook, T. D., & Campbell, D. T. (1979). *Quasi-experimentation: Design and analysis issues for field settings.* Chicago, IL: Rand McNally.

Cronbach, L. J. (1982). *Designing evaluations of educational and social programs.* San Francisco, CA: Jossey-Bass.

Donaldson, S. I. (2007). *Program theory-driven evaluation science: Strategies and applications.* New York, NY: Lawrence Erlbaum.

Donaldson, S. I., Christie, C. A., & Mark, M. M. (Eds.). (2008). *What counts as credible evidence in applied research and evaluation practice?* Newbury Park, CA: Sage.

Green, L. W., & Glasgow, R. E. (2006). Evaluating the relevance, generalization, and applicability of research: Issues in external validation and translation methodology. *Evaluation & the Health Professions, 29*(1), 126–153.

Greene, J. (2008). Evidence as "proof" and evidence as "inkling." In S. I. Donaldson, C. Christie, & M. M. Mark (Eds.), *What counts as credible evidence in applied research and evaluation practice?* Thousand Oaks, CA: Sage.

Guba, E. G., & Lincoln, Y. S. (1989). *Fourth generation evaluation.* Newbury Park, CA: Sage.

Huffman, D., & Lawrenz, F. (Eds.). (2006). *Critical issues in STEM evaluation.* San Francisco, CA: Jossey-Bass.

Lissitz, R. (2009). *The concept of validity: Revisions, new directions, and applications.* Charlotte, NC: Information Age Publishing.

Maxwell, J. A. (1992). Understanding and validity in qualitative research. *Harvard Educational Review, 62*(3), 279–300.

Messick, S. (1989). Validity. In R. Linn (Ed.), *Educational measurement* (3rd ed., pp. 13–103). New York, NY: American Council on Education/Macmillan.

Scriven, M. (2008). Demythologizing causation and evidence. In S. I. Donaldson, C. Christie, & M. M. Mark (Eds.), *What counts as credible evidence in applied research and evaluation practice?* (pp. 134–152). Thousand Oaks, CA: Sage.

Shadish, W. R., Cook, T. D., & Campbell, D. T. (2002). *Experimental and quasi-experimental designs for generalized causal inference.* Boston, MA: Houghton Mifflin.

Shadish, W. R., Cook, T. D., & Leviton, L. C. (1991). *Foundation of program evaluation: Theories of practice.* Newbury Park, CA: Sage.

Shadish, W. R., & Luellen, J. K. (2004). Donald Campbell: The accidental evaluator. In M. C. Alkin (Ed.), *Evaluation roots: Tracing theorists' views and influences* (pp. 80–87). Thousand Oaks, CA: Sage.

Wandersman, A., Duffy, J., Flaspohler, P., Noonan, R., Lubell, K., Stillman, L., et al. (2008). Bridging the gap between prevention research and practice: The interactive systems framework for dissemination and implementation. *American Journal of Community Psychology, 41*(3–4), 171–181.

HUEY T. CHEN is a senior evaluation scientist of the Air Pollution and Respiratory Health Branch at the Centers for Disease Control and Prevention (CDC).

STEWART I. DONALDSON is dean and professor of psychology at the Claremont Graduate University.

MELVIN M. MARK is professor and head of psychology at Penn State University.

Gargani, J., & Donaldson, S. I. (2011). What works for whom, where, why, for what, and when? Using evaluation evidence to take action in local contexts. In H. T. Chen, S. I. Donaldson, & M. M. Mark (Eds.), *Advancing validity in outcome evaluation: Theory and practice. New Directions for Evaluation, 130,* 17–30.

2

What Works for Whom, Where, Why, for What, and When? Using Evaluation Evidence to Take Action in Local Contexts

John Gargani, Stewart I. Donaldson

Abstract

This chapter describes a concrete process that stakeholders can use to make predictions about the future performance of programs in local contexts. Within the field of evaluation, the discussion of validity as it relates to outcome evaluation seems to be focused largely on questions of internal validity (Did it work?) with less emphasis on external validity (Will it work?). However, recent debates about the credibility of evaluation evidence have called attention to how evaluations can inform predictions about future performance. Using this as a starting point, we expand upon the traditional framework regarding external validity that is closely associated with Donald Campbell. The result is a process for making predictions and taking action that is collaborative, systematic, feasible, and transparent. © Wiley Periodicals, Inc., and the American Evaluation Association.

Introduction

Imagine that you were asked to choose between two crystal balls. The first can unerringly tell you whether a program *improved* the lives of past participants, and the second can unerringly tell you whether a program *will improve* the lives of future participants. If you are like most in our profession, the crystal ball that predicts the future is far more desirable because evaluation is action oriented—we engage the world in order to improve it. Descriptions of the past, whether to promote accountability or inform historical debate, would largely become irrelevant if we knew for certain the future consequences of policies and programs. Yet in spite of our desire to be forward looking, recent debates within the evaluation professional societies seem fixated on the past. In particular, we have spent an inordinate amount of time arguing, often with raised voices, about whether evaluations with experimental designs are the best way to describe the past performance of a program, all the while neglecting the ways in which we can shed more light on future performance using the methodologically diverse evaluations we actually produce. For example, the internal validity of experiments has been the focus of policy statements by the American Evaluation Association (AEA, 2003), the European Evaluation Society (EES, 2007), and Bickman et al. (2003); debates between Michael Scriven and Thomas Cook (Cook, Scriven, Coryn, & Evergreen, 2010) and Scriven and Mark Lipsey (Donaldson & Christie, 2005); and extended discussion by many contemporary evaluation scholars (Donaldson, Christie, & Mark, 2008). The external validity of evaluations, experimental or otherwise, has not seemed to generate the same level of attention and heated discourse in recent years.

The main purpose of this chapter is to shift the discussion of validity as it relates to outcome evaluation from the past to the future, from concepts of internal validity to those of external validity, and from the quality of evidence we can produce to how we can use the evidence we have to make predictions and take effective action. We begin by describing the recent debates about credible evidence that have dominated the professional landscape. Then we provide a brief overview of the traditional validity framework as it relates to external validity and discuss the applicability of the framework to modern evaluation practice. We conclude by suggesting how stakeholders can use evaluation evidence to make predictions that inform action in local contexts.

What Works? What Do You Mean?

Over the past 10 years, policymakers on both sides of the aisle have come to believe that evaluations should answer a now-ubiquitous question—what works? Bipartisan faith in our ability to answer the question is exemplified by the education policies of Presidents George W. Bush and Barack Obama. As different as these two leaders may be, both initiated large-scale policies— No Child Left Behind and Race to the Top, respectively—in which they used evaluation to help their administrations fund what works (Bush, 2001; Obama, 2009) instead of "fancy theories" (Bush, 2002), "what sounds good" (Bush, 2004), or "ideology" (Obama, 2008). The Bush administration was so confident that evaluation would produce credible evidence of effective programs that the U.S. Department of Education's Institute of Education Sciences created the What Works Clearinghouse to catalog and disseminate evaluation results (Institute of Education Sciences, n.d.). As a profession, this is the exactly the sort of role that we have long argued evaluation should play (Campbell, 1988), and the fact that it has been endorsed by Republicans and Democrats would seem to signal that the profession may have arrived.

Yet we wonder how evaluators can best answer the question "What works?" The question does not explicitly ask for a description of the past performance of a program (What *worked?*) or a prediction of future performance (What *will work?*). Rather it requires that the past and the future be addressed simultaneously, the former with evaluation results and the latter with a line of reasoning that connects past results to future action. Using the past to inform the future has many pitfalls, but it is made far more problematic because the question (What *works?*) suggests a false line of reasoning—to know past performance is to know future performance. This is what we typically mean when we assert that something works. If one turns the ignition key in an automobile and it starts, one may accurately state that the car works. By this we understand that it works today, it will almost certainly work tomorrow and the day after that, and it will work under a wide variety of conditions. A similar assertion cannot be made about programs because they famously do not perform consistently over time and across contexts. Thus the answer to the question "What works?" must always be a qualified answer, stipulating for whom, where, why, for what, and when the program will be effective. The challenge facing evaluators is therefore twofold—how to provide qualified answers and how to use them to construct lines of reasoning that yield reliable predictions about the future performance of programs in specific contexts.

This is a formidable challenge; we lack a systematic history of concern with making predictions of this sort, and no theory is available for researchers who want to ensure that their evaluations better inform future action (Shadish, Cook, & Campbell, 2002, p. 342). However, recent debates about what constitutes credible evidence have shed new light on how lines of reasoning connecting past results to future performance can be strengthened. The underlying premise of the debate is not controversial—the more credible the evidence produced by an evaluation, the more sound the conclusions based upon it. However, there is currently a fundamental disagreement in the field about what counts as credible evidence (see Donaldson et al., 2008). Although this dispute has an eerie similarity to the qualitative–quantitative Paradigm War of the 1970s and 1980s, the current Causal War is different in that it focuses largely on what constitutes scientifically based evaluation methods (Scriven, 2008). A central theme in the debate is whether or not randomized controlled trials (RCTs) are the best design—the so-called gold standard—or even a good design for producing credible evidence that answers the question "What works?"

Some evaluators argue that the problem is not whether evidence is credible, per se, but whether the evidence can be acted upon. In particular, by organizing evaluation resources around one small question—Does the program work?—they contend that evaluations can produce only one small answer (Greene, 2008). This answer may have some utility, but it is probably insufficient to guide the actions of policymakers at a national level, and it entirely misses the mark for the immediate stakeholders of a program. The people who work directly with programs or are directly affected by them want to know if a program will be effective in the local context in which they have the power to act.

Julnes and Rog (2008) noted that in order for evidence to be useful, it needs to be actionable as well as credible. In particular, it needs to be deemed appropriate for guiding actions in specific local contexts. We concur, and action in local contexts is our motivating consideration. The debate over evidence has, nonetheless, focused largely on its credibility, which has come to mean how persuasive it is to experts who embrace a traditional, quantitative research paradigm. We are, without apology, among those who are sympathetic to this paradigm, yet we worry that the debate has turned too tightly on how evidence quality relates to concepts of internal validity and efforts to prescribe a small number of preferred evaluation designs.

In an effort to shift the debate from credibility to action, we will make use of three concepts that require some clarification. *Validity*, the principal concept that we discuss, is both an argument and a warrant. Evaluators must make the case that the evaluation evidence they produce can be used in a particular way for a particular purpose; this is the argument for validity. When others use evaluation evidence in a given manner, they justify their action by citing a relevant validity argument that they accept; this is validity used as a warrant. Of course, evaluators may argue for one use and others may put evaluation evidence to different uses, which places the burden of making the argument upon the latter group. From this perspective, validity is not an on-or-off quality of the evaluation or a characteristic of evidence, but a responsibility shared by the evaluator and the user, a key point in our later discussion of alternatives.

There are many types of validity, and we are concerned with what has traditionally been called external validity and how it warrants *prediction*. By this we mean more than generalization, which is limited to concluding that programs replicated under similar circumstances will tend to produce similar results. Prediction entails using judgments about the past performance of particular programs in particular circumstances to make judgments about the future performance of different programs in different circumstances. It is the more difficult and, we believe, common task facing evaluators and stakeholders.

If one accepts an argument for external validity, made either by the evaluator or a user of the evaluation, one feels justified in using the results of a past evaluation to make certain predictions about the future results of other programs. However, each of us forms our own beliefs about the persuasiveness of the validity argument, and given our varied research traditions, tolerances for uncertainty, prior beliefs, personal stakes in programs, and evaluation approaches, consensus is the exception. In order to act on our predictions, we must somehow develop a *shared faith* in three things—the evaluation results we consider (a) are believable, (b) reflect the results of past programs, and (c) predict the future results of other programs. Faith in this sense is arrived at individually, but faith can only be acted upon collectively, which brings us back to the point that validity is a shared responsibility. The extent to which we share it and with whom we share it are key concerns of modern evaluation practice that differentiate it from traditional research.

The Traditional Validity Framework

Describing *the* traditional validity framework and how it relates to external validity is challenging because the framework continues to evolve after almost a century. The earliest versions of the framework promoted a belief that researchers could generalize their findings with greater confidence if their research had designs of a particular type. Over time, this perspective expanded, and, with respect to evaluation, now promotes a belief that users of evaluation (including but not limited to researchers) can make a wider range of inferences based on evaluations with a variety of designs. We describe the development of the framework, and in the next section discuss why, although it is useful, it does not constitute a complete solution to the challenges facing evaluators.

Pioneering Work

As early as 1923, McCall's *How to Experiment in Education* offered a comprehensive validity framework, albeit without using the word *validity*. It cataloged a series of experimental designs that could be used to determine the effectiveness of educational interventions, each of which was represented by letters separated by dashes, for example, IT-EF-FT for initial test (pretest), experimental factor (treatment), and final test (posttest), that foreshadowed the X-O diagrams so strongly associated with Campbell. McCall (1923) argued that experimentation should lead to the widespread adoption of more effective and efficient practices, but did not explain how experimental results could help bring this about. By the time Greenwood (1945) and Chapin (1947) presented their own systematic approaches to using experiments to evaluate social interventions, they recognized that focusing on designing a good experiment often detracted from findings that could be applied widely, what Greenwood (p. 93) called trading significance for accuracy. Again, they offered few details about how experiments should promote action, but Chapin (pp. vii–viii, 187–189) vigorously argued that the subsequent success of a program could only be assessed if researchers purposefully replicated their experiments (something that he acknowledged was a rarity).

NEW DIRECTIONS FOR EVALUATION • DOI: 10.1002/ev

External Validity and Generalizability

One of the great contributions that Campbell made was that he reorganized and expanded upon this nascent body of work, creating a more coherent, correct, and useful framework. At its heart is the distinction between internal validity and external validity (Campbell, 1957). The former provides a basis for believing a study's result, which takes the form of a quantitative estimate of the actual treatment–control contrast given all of the particulars of a study's circumstances. The latter provides a reason to believe that a study's result is generalizable, which is to say that one can expect a similar result if the study is replicated under similar circumstances. We use the term *circumstances* as a catchall for everything that could be different between two replications of a study, in particular persons, settings, treatments, outcomes, and times, which are the five dimensions that Campbell and his peers most explicitly addressed (Cook, 1993; Cronbach, 1982).

Random sampling provided the strongest (and some argued only) justification for generalization, but Campbell soon conceded that the problems associated with it were largely insurmountable (sampling persons was difficult; sampling times impossible; see Campbell, 1986, p. 71). This led him to suggest an alternative logic for generalization that was based on what he called the principle of proximal similarity—that scientists generalize with most confidence to applications most similar to the setting of the original research. He acknowledged that this was something of punt, a "metatheoretical basis for justifying a seemingly atheoretical rationale and approach to the generalization of findings" (p. 73). The irony is that although he is considered by some to be an unwavering proponent of quantitative methods, Campbell argued for a wholly qualitative approach to generalization in which, "the principle of proximal similarity is normally (and it should be) implemented on the basis of expert intuition" (p. 76).

Construct Validity

The crisp distinction promised by the labels *internal* and *external* never fully materialized, in part because of a long-standing confusion over what we refer to as shared faith that evaluation results reflect program results. This is well illustrated by an example that Campbell used in 1957 and returned to in 1986—placebos. If knowledge that one is being treated is considered an unwanted part of an actual treatment–control contrast, what he lyrically referred to as "the total X stimulus complex," then we can "purify X" by including multiple treatment–control contrasts, such as a nothing control versus a placebo-only control versus the pill-based treatment under investigation. We can do this at the time of the original study or in subsequent "transition experiments"; either way purifying X was intended to qualify the argument for external validity more fully. What many found counterintuitive is that purifying X has no effect on internal validity (all else being equal). So an experiment with three conditions (like the one described above) offers no potential benefit in terms of internal validity compared to an experiment with only two of the three conditions, even though the former offers a more useful result.

Campbell (1986) recognized that lumping the substantive interpretation of the treatment under the heading of external validity was confusing, so he endeavored along with Cook (Cook & Campbell, 1979) to introduce what is now called construct validity to set the matter straight. The hope was that when researchers asserted, "It works," this new form of validity would help everyone understand what was meant by *it*. The precise nature of the external-construct distinction crystallized slowly; Cook and Campbell organized threats to external and construct validity one way in 1976, moved two threats from the former to the latter in 1979 (p. 82), and Shadish et al. used a functional approach to reorganize them again in 2002 (pp. 467–468). Although these niceties are now well settled, construct validity still has the effect of muddying the internal–external dichotomy. This may be why it has received far less attention than it deserves and seems to be perceived as an awkward third wheel rather than the stabilizing third leg of the stool.

Generalization More Broadly Defined

As the framework evolved, the uses subsumed under the label of generalization expanded. In particular, Cook (1993) and later Shadish et al. (2002) suggested five principles that support generalization, interpolation, and extrapolation, which collectively get closer to what we mean by prediction. In line with Campbell's perspective, these authors argued that generalizing from a source (the past) to a target (the future) is logically warranted when the populations, treatments, outcomes, settings, and times of the source and target are: (a) very similar (Principle 1: Surface Similarity); (b) different but do not influence the effectiveness of the program (Principle 2: Ruling Out Irrelevancies); (c) different, influence the effectiveness of the program, but are identified and can be avoided or controlled (Principle 3: Making Discriminations); (d) manipulatable in such a way that program effectiveness can be controlled or predicted, as it can be when there is a known dose-response relationship (Principle 4: Interpolation and Extrapolation); or (e) described by a well-crafted causal theory that can be used to explicate results (Principle 5: Causal Explanation).

Evaluators can discover how strongly these principles hold by designing their evaluations in ways that allow them to analyze variation in results. That variation can be naturally occurring (men versus women) or purposefully introduced (ensuring a range of ages or using more than one version of the treatment); explored in a single study setting (one program) or across many settings (multiple programs); and manifested all at once (multisite evaluations) or sequentially (replication). In short, if one can design an evaluation that estimates how variation in circumstances (populations, treatments, etc.) relates to variation in results, one has a logically sound basis for controlling or predicting future results across (and at times beyond) the range of circumstances considered.

Applicability of the Traditional Framework to Modern Evaluation Practice

As evaluation developed as a field, a number of prominent evaluators began questioning the applicability of the traditional framework to evaluation practice. For example, *naturalistic generalization* (Stake, 1978), *reproducibility* (Cronbach, 1982), and *transferability* (Guba & Lincoln, 1989) were all intended to replace, or at least augment, traditional concepts of generalization and external validity. None of these alternatives took root, and most practicing evaluators are probably unaware of them. However, they reflect a persistent sentiment within the field that the traditional framework does not fully serve evaluation as it is really practiced. Some of these criticisms stem from fundamental differences about how research should be conducted, and those who make them are unlikely to be satisfied by anything short of revolutionary change. On the other hand, there are evaluators, like Cronbach, with more conventional views regarding research methods, who have also perceived a misfit. It is from this perspective that we explore how evaluators can more fully reconcile the traditional framework with modern evaluation practice.

First, the traditional framework is strongly linked with the concept of generalization, when what is more relevant is prediction. Although generalization has developed a more expansive meaning over time, it does not fully encompass how stakeholders actually use evaluation evidence. For example, when stakeholders design innovative programs or address newly emerging social issues, they are making predictions with evidence that is too thin for the five principles to be applied as scientists would, if they can be applied at all.

Second, the traditional framework was intended to help researchers generalizing the results of experimental research, not stakeholders predicting the performance of programs in specific, local contexts. The former can be a proxy for the latter, but an imperfect one because treatment protocols, the primary interest of experimentalists, are tidier, narrower, and more replicable than programs, which entail staffing, funding, and myriad other organizational operations performed in idiosyncratic contexts. Ideally, we would like to connect the past effectiveness of treatments to the future effectiveness of programs in ways that better support action and are not limited to the use of experimental results.

Third, dependence on expert intuition is troubling. Although this is only suggested in the absence of an empirical or rigorous basis for generalization, this is arguably the most common situation. Relying on experts can easily be construed as taking control away from stakeholders and giving it to those who are not directly impacted by the program. One can avoid this by defining expert as stakeholder, and Campbell may well have endorsed this definition, but the more serious problem is that regardless of who is in control, characterizing the judgment of similarity as intuition implies that it is unconscious, mystical, and opaque. What we want instead is a process that is intentional, logical, and transparent.

Fourth, if the purpose of an evaluation is to answer some variation of the question "What works?", it is important to remember that what works depends on what matters. The values that lead one person, group, or organization to declare success may lead others to declare failure or shrug their shoulders with uncertainty. Differences in values are a healthy part of the messy democratic process, yet they do not fit easily into the orderly confines of the traditional framework developed by experimenters who are far more like-minded than the stakeholders, policymakers, and general public they serve.

Fifth, the traditional framework assumes that programs are static, well documented, replicable entities. The reality is that programs need only be developed to the level that satisfies funding requirements, which is far from the level of detail that would allow them to be implemented with consistency. Thus, any particular implementation of a program is an unstable amalgam of intention, improvisation, responsive local adaptation, ongoing improvement efforts, funding requirements, and staff competence. Given this, we would like to take into account not only random treatment variation, but variation that is intentional, continuous, and potentially beneficial.

Toward a More Systematic Process for Making Predictions

The decision to implement a program depends in large part on whether decision makers predict it will succeed or fail. Traditionally, this prediction is based on either a narrow form of generalization (expecting similar results in similar circumstances) or a more expansive form (interpolating or extrapolating results from theoretically or empirically established patterns of covariance). However, neither similar circumstances nor established patterns of covariance are commonly found in practice. So, how should these predictions be made? We suggest that when traditional approaches cannot be applied, stakeholders should make predictions using the systematic, collaborative process we describe. We have no empirical evidence to suggest that it is the best way to make predictions of program performance specifically. However, there is empirical evidence that systematic approaches such as these can improve predictions generally (see for example Dawes, 1979). In addition, the process is feasible, transparent, and follows from the ideas introduced by Campbell that we have built upon in this chapter.

The first step in the process is for stakeholders to surface a program theory. A great deal has been written about how to do this (Chen, 1990; Donaldson, 2007; Knowlton & Phillips, 2009) and how a program theory should reflect a shared understanding of which outcomes stakeholders hope to achieve and how the various characteristics of the program, participants, and setting are expected to interact to bring about those outcomes (see Donaldson, 2001, 2007; Donaldson & Gooler, 2003). With their program theory in hand, stakeholders review evaluations of candidate programs. The purpose of the review is to determine whether stakeholders share a faith in the believability of the evaluation results, the relevance of the results to the programs that were evaluated, and predictions based on the results. Believability is addressed when stakeholders answer the question, "Are some or all of the evaluation findings related to program effectiveness credible?" (See Appendix for a data-collection form that scaffolds this process.) Relevance is addressed by answering the questions, "Do the evaluation results reasonably represent the results of the program that was evaluated?" and "Does the evaluation provide evidence about some or all of the outcomes in our program theory?" These deceptively simple questions may require that stakeholders engage in considerable discussion before they agree on answers.

If stakeholders answer "no" to any of the questions, the evaluation under consideration will not inform predictions and stakeholders should look to other evaluations for evidence that will serve their needs. If they answer "yes" to all three questions, then stakeholders dig deeper, establishing the extent to which they believe past results predict future results. They do this by considering each outcome in their program theory, summarizing the evaluation evidence, indicating whether they consider it credible, and judging whether the level or quality of the observed outcome meets their definition of success. Then they consider for whom, where, when, and why the past program was implemented, describe the similarities and differences between these contextual factors and the ones they specified for their own program theory, and predict whether implementing the program in their local context would yield results that were better than, the same as, or worse than prior results. This is accompanied by a brief explanation of the logic underlying the predictions.

At the end of the process, if there is a consistent pattern of prior evaluation results meeting the current standard of success, and judgments that future circumstances will lead to the same or better results, the decision to implement the program becomes quite easy. More likely, the results will be mixed, leading to more discussion and debate, and possibly a decision to modify an existing program, combine elements of several programs, or design an entirely new program. The critical feature for us is that the final predictions, the actions that follow from them, and the logic underlying both are well documented. If that is the case, it becomes possible to monitor programs as they are implemented and make midcourse corrections that increase the likelihood of success.

Conclusions

We care about validity because it reduces risky leaps of faith to more manageable hops of faith. In the end, however, it always comes down to faith—faith in the results of past evaluations, faith that those results represent the effectiveness of the programs that were evaluated, and faith that past results are a reasonable basis for predicting future success. For us the debate is not exclusively about how we come to have faith. In fact, we have worked hard to dodge the question of how we come to have faith in past evaluation results. That falls under the traditional heading of internal validity and has consumed a disproportionate amount of our profession's time and attention. Instead, we have focused on how we use the faith we have to make predictions about the future effectiveness of programs in ways that can help us take effective action.

Our argument is premised on a belief that the quality of evaluation evidence at our disposal will, at least for the near term, remain at a level that is lower than we desire. Consequently, meaningful improvements in how we act can only come from improvements in how we use the evidence at hand. We have suggested a systematic process for using evidence to make predictions that inform action, but we are not wedded to the details of that process. What we seek is a transparent, collective, and logical mechanism for taking action, and a commitment to monitor and adjust those actions over time.

We have also argued for placing the work of prediction into the hands of stakeholders. Without the inclusion and leadership of stakeholders, the values and concerns of those closest to programs will not be adequately addressed. We acknowledge that the sort of comprehensive, local deliberation that we suggest may be something of an impractical, romantic notion. It is subject to the same barrier that obstructs strategic planning, collaborative goal setting, and off-site training—it takes time and attention away from busy professionals. Yet we believe it is worth promoting, if only to contrast to the current state of evidence-based practice. From our vantage point, we have watched with disappointment as programs are hurriedly "designed" by desperate grant writers and program directors in the middle of the night as they make every attempt to be responsive to a request for proposals. The programs that emerge are called evidence-based because evidence was used to justify them. But we reject this "if you cite it must be right" mind-set that tempts many to troll contradictory research findings in order to pluck the few that help them make their case, sadly lending credence to the old saying, "Program evaluation is evaluation that supports my program."

But there is another adage that warns that we predict the future from the past at our own peril. This one, however, is less accurate, because when we make predictions about programs and policies, it is others, often the most vulnerable, who are put in peril and suffer if we are wrong. If we cannot consistently depend on evidence of higher quality, we can at least be smarter about how we use the evidence we have. And we can ensure that those who are most directly affected by programs are not treated as "others" but are among those reviewing the evidence, making predictions, and acting on them. Evaluations serve many different groups and they employ a variety of theoretical stances, practical approaches, and research methods. The profession should reflect this reality, and it is what motivated us to suggest a group process that does not depend on endorsing any one evaluation approach. However, our suggestion is not a condemnation of the traditional validity framework, but, we hope, a testament to how fundamentally sound it is that it can support extensions and adaptations of this kind.

References

American Evaluation Association. (2003). *American Evaluation Association response to U.S. Department of Education notice of proposed priority, Federal Register RIN 1890-ZA00, November 4, 2003 "Scientifically Based Evaluation Methods"*. Retrieved from http://www.eval.org/doestatement.htm

Bickman, L., Boruch, R. F., Cook, T. D., Cordray, D. S., Henry, G. T., Lipsey, M. W., Rossi, P. H., et al. (2003, December 3). Not the AEA statement [EVALTALK electronic mailing list message]. Retrieved from http://bama.ua.edu/archives/evaltalk.html

Bush, G. W. (2001). *President commends Congress for passage of landmark education bill*. Retrieved from http://georgewbush-whitehouse.archives.gov/news/releases/2001/12/20011218.html

Bush, G. W. (2002). *President highlights progress made in education reform*. Retrieved from http://georgewbush-whitehouse.archives.gov/news/releases/2002/09/20020904-6.html

Bush, G. W. (2004). *President Bush discusses progress in education in St. Louis*. Retrieved from http://georgewbush-whitehouse.archives.gov/news/releases/2004/01/20040105-2.html

Campbell, D. T. (1957). Factors relevant to the validity of experiments in social settings. *Psychological Bulletin, 54*(4), 297–312.

Campbell, D. T. (1986). Relabeling internal and external validity for the applied social sciences. In W. M. K. Trochim (Ed.), *Advances in quasi-experimental design and analysis. New Directions for Program Evaluation, 31*, 67–77.

Campbell, D. T. (1988). The experimenting society. In E. S. Overman (Ed.), *Methodology and epistemology for social science: Selected papers* (pp. 290–314). Chicago: University of Chicago Press.

Chapin, F. S. (1947). *Experimental designs in sociological research*. New York: Harper and Brothers.

Chen, H. T. (1990). *Theory-driven evaluations*. Newbury Park, CA: Sage.

Cook, T. D. (1993). A quasi-sampling theory of the generalization of causal relationships. In L. B. Sechrest & A. G. Scott (Eds.), *Understanding causes and generalizing about them. New Directions for Evaluation, 57*, 39–82.

Cook, T. D., & Campbell, D. T. (1979). *Quasi-experimentation: Design & analysis issues for field settings*. Boston: Houghton Mifflin.

Cook, T. D., Scriven, M., Coryn, C. L. S., & Evergreen, S. D. H. (2010). Contemporary thinking about causation in evaluation: A dialogue with Tom Cook and Michael Scriven. *American Journal of Evaluation, 31*(1), 105–117.

Cronbach, L. J. (1982). *Designing evaluations of educational and social programs*. San Francisco: Jossey-Bass.

Dawes, R. (1979). The robust beauty of improper linear models in decision making. *American Psychologist, 34*(7), 571–582.

Donaldson, S. I. (2001). Mediator and moderator analysis in program development. In S. Sussman (Ed.), *Handbook of program development for health behavior research and practice* (pp. 470–496). Newbury Park, CA: Sage.

Donaldson, S. I. (2007). *Program theory-driven evaluation science*. Mahwah, NJ: Lawrence Erlbaum Associates.

Donaldson, S. I., & Christie, C. A. (2005). The 2004 Claremont Debate: Lipsey versus Scriven. Determing causality in program evaluation and applied research: Should experimental evidence be the gold standard? *Journal of Multidisciplinary Evaluation, 3*, 60–77.

Donaldson, S. I., Christie, C. A., & Mark, M. M. (2008). *What counts as credible evidence in applied research and evaluation practice?* Newbury Park, CA: Sage.

Donaldson, S. I., & Gooler, L. E. (2003). Theory-driven evaluation in action: Lessons from a $20 million statewide work and health initiative. *Evaluation and Program Planning, 26*, 355–366.

European Evaluation Society. (2007). *EES statement: The importance of a methodologically diverse approach to impact evaluation—specifically with respect to development aid and development interventions.* Retrieved from http://www.europeanevaluation.org/download/?id=1969403

Greene, J. C. (2008). Evidence as "proof" and evidence as "inkling." In S. I. Donaldson, C. A. Christie, & M. M. Mark (Eds.), *What counts as credible evidence in applied research and evaluation practice?* Newbury Park, CA: Sage.

Greenwood, E. (1945). *Experimental sociology: A study in method.* New York: King's Crown Press.

Guba, E. G., & Lincoln, Y. S. (1989). *Fourth generation evaluation.* Newbury Park, CA: Sage.

Institute of Education Sciences. (n.d.). *About us.* Retrieved from http://ies.ed.gov/ncee/wwc/aboutus/

Julnes, G., & Rog, D. (2008). Evaluation methods for producing actionable evidence: Contextual influences on adequacy and appropriateness of method choice. In S. I. Donaldson, C. A. Christie, & M. M. Mark (Eds.), *What counts as credible evidence in applied research and evaluation practice?* Newbury Park, CA: Sage.

Knowlton, L. W., & Phillips, C. C. (2009). *The logic model guidebook: Better strategies for great results.* Thousand Oaks, CA: Sage.

McCall, W. A. (1923). *How to experiment in education.* New York: MacMillan.

Obama, B. H. (2008). *Full text of Obama's education speech (What's possible for our children).* Retrieved from http://www.denverpost.com/news/ci_9405199

Obama, B. H. (2009). *Remarks by the President on education.* Retrieved from http://www.whitehouse.gov/the-press-office/remarks-president-department-education

Scriven, M. (2008). Demythologizing causation and evidence. In S. I. Donaldson, C. A. Christie, & M. M. Mark, *What counts as credible evidence in applied research and evaluation practice?* Newbury Park, CA: Sage.

Shadish, W. R., Cook, T. D., & Campbell, D. T. (2002). *Experimental and quasi-experimental designs for generalized causal inference.* Boston: Houghton Mifflin.

Stake, R. E. (1978). The case study method in social inquiry. *Educational Researcher, 7*(2), 5–8.

JOHN GARGANI is president of Gargani + Company, Inc., a program design and evaluation firm located in Berkeley, California.

STEWART I. DONALDSON is dean and professor of psychology at the Claremont Graduate University.

Appendix: Scaffolded Questions for Evaluation Evidence Review

Believability

Are some or all of the evaluation findings related to program effectiveness credible? Yes/No

Relevance

Do the evaluation results reasonably represent the results of the program that was evaluated? Yes/No

Does the evaluation provide evidence about some or all of the outcomes in our program theory? Yes/No

Prediction

Outcome 1	Outcome 2	Outcome 3
Summary of findings:	Summary of findings:	And so on . . .
The findings ARE NOT/ARE credible	The findings ARE NOT/ARE credible	And so on . . .
This result DOES NOT/DOES meet our standard	This result DOES NOT/DOES meet our standard	

What is the plausible effect of similarities and differences on outcomes?

	Similarities	Differences	Outcome 1	Outcome 2	Outcome 3
For whom? How do past participants compare to our participants?			WORSE/SAME/BETTER than prior result or CANNOT SAY Because . . .	WORSE/SAME/BETTER than prior result or CANNOT SAY Because . . .	And so on . . . / And so on . . .
Where and when? How does the past setting compare to our setting?			WORSE/SAME/BETTER than prior result or CANNOT SAY Because . . .	And so on . . .	And so on . . .
Why? How does the past program theory compare to our program theory?			WORSE/SAME/BETTER than prior result or CANNOT SAY Because . . .	And so on . . .	And so on . . .

Mark, M. M. (2011). New (and old) directions for validity concerning generalizability. In H. T. Chen, S. I. Donaldson, & M. M. Mark (Eds.), *Advancing validity in outcome evaluation: Theory and practice. New Directions for Evaluation, 130*, 31–42.

3

New (and Old) Directions for Validity Concerning Generalizability

Melvin M. Mark

Abstract

The author addresses the issue of generalizability as it arises in outcome evaluations. Methods for enhancing knowledge about generalizability in the Campbellian tradition are briefly reviewed. Recommendations are made for future practice and promising areas of future advancement regarding understanding generalizability in outcome evaluation. © Wiley Periodicals, Inc., and the American Evaluation Association.

Program evaluation would be a historical exercise unless one assumes some ability to generalize from evaluation findings to settings, times, and program participants other than those directly observed in the evaluation (Cronbach, 1982). Although a range of opinions exists, most evaluators apparently hope or presume that evaluation findings have *some* implications beyond the persons, settings, and times of the evaluation. It appears that at the very least, evaluators hope that evaluation findings have meaningful implications for decisions about the same program in the near future in the same setting. Likewise, at least some stakeholders appear to assume a degree of generalizability of evaluation findings. For example, how often would funders allocate resources to evaluation if they assumed that it was a purely historical exercise with no generalizability to the times, clients, and setting(s) in which they are interested?

This chapter addresses the issue of generalizability as it arises in "outcome evaluations," particularly evaluation studies that use experiments, quasi-experiments, and/or other methods to try to assess whether and to what extent a program (or other evaluand) helps bring about a change in one or more outcomes of interest. Other kinds of evaluations can of course be preferable, depending on factors such as a program's stage of development, the state of knowledge about the program (and programs like it), and the information needs and potential uses of various stakeholder groups. Nevertheless, outcome evaluations can be important and are the focus here. The validity framework and related ideas from Donald Campbell and his associates have been influential among a segment of outcome evaluators, and so that framework receives attention here.

Generalizability and External Validity

Campbell and his colleagues have offered three major versions of the taxonomy of validity types of which external validity is a part. In the initial version, Campbell and Stanley (1963, p. 5) contrasted internal and external validity. Internal validity was described as "the basic minimum without which any experiment is uninterpretable: Did in fact the experimental treatments make a difference in this specific experimental instance?" External validity, in contrast "asks the question of *generalizability*: 'To what populations, settings, treatment variables, and measurement variables can this effect be generalized?'"

Cook and Campbell (1979) distinguished statistical conclusion validity, which involves conclusions about the covariation between treatment and outcome, from internal validity, which involves conclusions about whether a causal relationship exists between the treatment-as-implemented and the outcome-as-measured in the particular setting observed. Cook and Campbell also divided Campbell and Stanley's external validity into two categories. One of these, construct validity, focuses on the validity of labels used for the treatment and outcome (e.g., is it accurate to label the program as implemented *cognitive behavioral therapy* and the outcome as measured *depression*?). Cook and Campbell's construct validity involves generalization, specifically "the question: 'Can I generalize from this one [research] operation or set of operations to a referent construct?'" (1979, p. 39). External validity involves the validity of conclusions "about the generalizability of a causal relationship to and across populations of persons, setting, and times" (p. 39).

Shadish, Cook, and Campbell (2002) use similar definitions of statistical conclusion and internal validity, while modifying the definitions of construct and external validity. Their construct validity refers to the "validity of inference about the higher order constructs that represent sampling particulars." In contrast, their external validity refers to "whether the causal relationship holds over variation in persons, settings, treatments, and measurement variables." Cook and Campbell's construct validity applied only to treatments and outcomes, with external validity applying only to persons, settings, and times. In contrast, Shadish et al. apply both forms of validity to all these elements of an inference (treatments, outcomes, persons, settings, and times). Construct validity in this formulation is a somewhat narrower inference, involving the match between study operations and the higher-order labels used (e.g., by the evaluator) to describe the preceding elements (which can be considered apart from the treatment effect). External validity is a broader generalization, involving whether the causal relationship varies across differences in persons, settings, times, treatments, or outcomes. (Compare Mark, 1986 on the issue of level of generalization as an issue in different validity typologies. From that perspective, internal validity would involve the lowest level of inference, referring to research operations rather than to more abstract and use-relevant labels.)

The conception of external validity used here corresponds most closely to the Cook and Campbell (1979) approach. However, I often refer instead to validity regarding generalizability. This is because of the different referents for the term external validity and because of the potential confusion that Reichardt (this issue) notes regarding the meaning of the term external validity.

Because of space limitations, it is not possible here to review alternative framings of the issue of generalizability beyond the evolving Campbellian tradition. These would include Cronbach's (1982) formulation of external validity in terms of the accurate labeling of elements in a causal statement (also see Reichardt, 2006), as well as a range of views more strongly associated with qualitative methods, such as transferability and situated or natural generalization (Guba & Lincoln, 1989; Maxwell, 1992; Stake, 2004b). This chapter focuses on the soundness of conclusions about the extent to which one can (and the circumstances under which one cannot) reasonably generalize from the findings of outcome evaluation—a concern often associated with external validity.

Enhancing Knowledge About Generalizability in the Campbellian Tradition

Drawing on Campbell and Stanley (1963), Cook and Campbell (1979) listed three threats to external validity. These are the (statistical) interaction of the treatment with characteristics of (a) individuals, (b) settings, or (c) times. In short, these threats involve the possibility that the treatment effect differs as a function of variation in these three elements (e.g., male versus female clients, or urban versus rural settings). Cook and Campbell identify three different sampling models that can be used to increase external validity: random sampling for representativeness, which provides a formal justification for generalizing, but is often infeasible and sometimes inconceivable (e.g., sampling past and future times); deliberate sampling for heterogeneity, for example, comparing effects across subsamples that vary on presumably important factors; and impressionistic modal instances, that is, selection of cases thought to be most like those to which one wishes to generalize.

New Directions for Evaluation • DOI: 10.1002/ev

For construct validity, a longer list of threats (e.g., monomethod bias, experimenter expectancies) is provided. Avoiding these threats enhances construct validity, but the key construct-validity issue involves (a) adequately explicating the relevant treatment and outcome constructs and (b) ensuring that the research operations "fit" the constructs. Cook and Campbell also note that for both external and construct validity, replication is perhaps the key means of enhancement.

Arguably the most notable expansion regarding generalization in Shadish et al. (2002) is the specification of five principles, drawn from Cook (1990) and thought to underlie efforts to generalize. These are: *surface similarity*, the apparent similarity between research operations and the more abstract target of generalization; *ruling out irrelevancies*, demonstration that a particular attribute (e.g., participant gender) does not change a conclusion; *making discriminations*, that is, finding factors that do limit a generalization; *interpolation and extrapolation*, that is, estimating the unobserved by projecting the findings based on known observations (e.g., estimating that effects for middle socioeconomic status, or SES, clients will be between those of low and high SES participants); and *causal explanation*, the development and testing of explanatory models for the causal relationship. Shadish et al. discuss the application of each of these principles in general. They also consider a variety of potential methods for enhancing generalization in relation to these principles, with these methods including the three sampling models from Cook and Campbell, narrative reviews, and meta-analyses. (As an aside, Mark, 1986, had suggested that three principles underlie methods that strengthen a generalization, a similarity principle, a robustness principle, and an explanation principle; the three and five principle models can be compared, but are not here.)

Campbell and colleagues are sometimes criticized for contributing to an overemphasis on internal and underemphasis on external validity in evaluation. This criticism in part draws on Campbell and Stanley's oft-quoted reference to internal validity as the sine qua non. However, Campbell himself contended that such criticism is "in a historical sense at least, wrong. Who, after all, introduced the great emphasis on, itemized all the threats to, and assembled the controls for external validity?" (1984, pp. 35–36). Such criticism also ignores the expanding attention to external validity across the three major books on design coauthored by Campbell, including the Shadish et al. focus on five principles for generalization (see related discussion in Chapter 1 of this issue). Nevertheless, expanded attention to generalizability in typical *evaluation practice* seems warranted.

Diverging Traditions in Evaluation

House (2002) argued that three different traditions in evaluation evolved in response to the limited use of early outcome evaluations, which in turn may have resulted from problems of generalizability: (a) more qualitative approaches, (b) meta-analysis, and (c) the theory-driven evaluation approach. The approaches tend to differ in terms of aspirations and beliefs about generalizability. Advocates of (program) theory-driven evaluation aspire to understand underlying mechanisms, knowledge of which can presumably inform decisions about where generalization is and is not called for (Chen, 2005; Donaldson, 2007; see also Mark, 1986; Shadish et al., 2002). Similarly, with meta-analysis used as a basis for evaluative conclusions, an argument can be made that this method provides a relatively good basis for generalization (or for identifying the limits of generalization). (Shadish et al., 2002 provide a detailed discussion about meta-analysis and generalization.) In contrast, some evaluations, typically of a more qualitative bent, eschew the aspiration of drawing wide generalizations. Instead, they view evaluation findings as locally situated, providing potential lessons that can help make experience-wise local actors smarter about the choices they face (e.g., Stake, 1978, 2004b)—a more limited form of generalization—from the specifics observed in the evaluation to at least somewhat different future circumstances.

Recommendations for Future Practice and for Areas of Future Development

There are several potentially fruitful directions for better supporting conclusions about generalizability in evaluation. Some are relatively new, whereas others are old but worthy of more widespread attention (with apologies, space limitations preclude careful citations to all the precursors of ideas presented here). Some of the suggestions primarily involve refinement of current practice, whereas others entail further methodological and analytic advances in service of subsequent practice.

Increase Attention to Extant Principles of and Methods for Generalization

Within the Campbellian tradition, Shadish et al. (2002), drawing in part on Cook (1990), provide the most detailed discussion of external validity. This includes extensive consideration of the five principles listed earlier and of specific techniques that can enhance knowledge about the basis for and limits to generalizability. None of these, alone or in combination, provide a foolproof guarantee that conclusions about generalizability will be completely accurate. However, they can improve on much of evaluation practice. For example, an evaluation report might include discussion of which principles of generalization support an evaluative conclusion, as implemented via what methods, as well as of the limits that remain. Recommendations for future evaluations could be given in relation to the strength of support for generalizations. One consequence might be the reduced application of supposed gold standard methods, rather than the consideration of validity priorities in light of the existing evidence base.

Stakeholder Input Regarding Target of Generalization

A potential future direction involves the greater use of systematic stakeholder processes to understand better the expected scope and nature of future generalization. Stakeholder involvement is commonplace in contemporary evaluation practice, in service of a range of tasks (Patton, 2008). Some of these relate to generalization, at least indirectly, as when intended users establish an intended evaluation use (Patton, 2008), or when stakeholders contribute to the development of a program theory that includes possible moderators of the program's effectiveness. Nevertheless, more widespread and more focused attention to stakeholders' views about generalizability seems warranted. This suggestion bears a relationship to Chen's suggestion of more "bottom up" approaches to validity (Chen, 2010; Chen & Garbe, this issue).

Echoing the alternative ways that utilization-focused and theory-driven evaluation approaches already address generalizability, two topics could be addressed with stakeholders. One is the *desired scope of generalizability*. For instance, imagine a school-based intervention being conducted in a large city's school district, with the goal being to increase the interest of middle-school children in science, technology, engineering, and mathematics (STEM) fields. Are stakeholders interested in conclusions about the school district as a whole? In program effects for particular subgroups of children within the school district? Are findings to be applied to other large urban school districts? To the state, or to the country as a whole? What is the anticipated time frame for application of the findings? Next year, when a decision is to be made about district-wide implementations? A short time frame during which the educational environment is expected to be relatively stable? A near term during which major changes, such as revisions to textbooks and curricula, are expected to follow from federal mandates for a common set of requirements across states? A longer term over which change is expected but the details of that change cannot be specified?

With a clearer sense of the specific scope of generalization that (various groups of) stakeholders seek, the evaluator might be able to do a better job in designing the evaluation, in seeking supplementary information, and in discussing limitations. For example, imagine that this is the one large city in a generally rural state, and yet application to the state overall is sought. With this target of generalizability clarified, the evaluator might seek to include one or more schools from typical districts outside the city. Or analyses and discussion might highlight a specific school or subgroup that is more representative of the rest of the state. Additionally, the evaluator might be able to identify other literature that is informative about the generalizability of study findings to sites across the state.

Stakeholder Input Regarding Potential Moderators

Stakeholders should also be asked to address a second topic, that is, their *understanding of the potential moderators of program effectiveness*. What factors do they think would make the program more effective or less effective? What variations in implementation, participant characteristics, aspects of the local context, and potential changes in the broader environment do stakeholders expect will affect program effectiveness? (Stakeholders might also be asked to identify expected mediators, that is, the interim changes they expect to result from the program and to lead to the longer-term outcomes of interest.) Stakeholders' perceptions need not be the only source of hypotheses about moderators. Also, they should be considered as hypotheses until they are tested. Still, stakeholder input on this topic probably is not solicited as often and in as much detail as it should be, with the exception of some theory-driven evaluation.

Explicit questioning of stakeholders about moderators could help guide the design of individual evaluations. For example, if the evaluator learns that stakeholders believe that parental education will moderate the effectiveness of a school-based STEM program, then efforts can be made to measure that variable and test it as a moderator. Even if a given factor cannot be included in the evaluation, the evaluator may be able to draw on other related research and theory to inform efforts to generalize. Attending to stakeholders' beliefs about likely moderators may have another potential benefit: Credibility about potential use may increase.

Developing a model of multiple stakeholders' beliefs might even help within traditions that eschew aspirations of wide generalizability. Take Stake's responsive evaluation tradition, in which "The evaluator should provide experiential accounts of program activity so that readers of the report can, through naturalistic generalization, arrive at their own judgments of quality in addition to those the evaluator provides" (Stake, 2004a, p. 215). Naturalistic generalization is "the act of drawing broad conclusions [i.e., generalizing] primarily from personal or vicarious experience, rather than from formal knowledge, however obtained" (Stake, 2004b, p. 174). Just as an evaluation report should, a listing of the factors that other relevant stakeholders think might moderate treatment effects should help potential evaluation users "do their own thinking" while "help[ing] them do it well" (Stake, 2004b, p. 175).

Research on Stakeholders' Beliefs About Generalizability

If over time enough evaluations elicited stakeholder input about the desired targets of generalization and expected moderators, and if the results were explicitly reported, synthesis across multiple evaluations could prove useful. For example, we might be able to develop models of stakeholder groups' preferred targets of generalizability. For instance, do stakeholders overall, or particular stakeholder groups, strongly prefer local, short-term targets for generalization? Or do they have in mind wider and longer-term application of evaluation results?

Rather than wait for reported stakeholder input about generalizability across multiple evaluations to synthesize, another approach could be taken.

That is, the issue of stakeholder preferences and mental models regarding generalizability could be a focus of research on evaluation.

Expand the Scope of Program Theory

At present, theory-driven evaluation focuses on theories of the program (or more generally, the evaluand). Such evaluations commonly include building and testing a model of the mediation and moderation of program effects and, to a lesser extent, program implementation. When potential moderators are specified, this obviously has relevance to tests that can enhance generalizability. However, the theories of theory-driven evaluation are primarily ones relevant to the translation of program operations into long-term outcomes. For example, social–psychologically based theories involving norms, intentions, anticipated outcomes, and the like may supply the potential mediators for a program aimed at changes in health behavior.

There is much less attention to "translational" theories, and relatedly to theories of culture and local context. For example, if the core program theory involves changing perceived norms, a translational question involves how one can effectively modify perceived norms in the circumstances in which the program is being implemented (see Mark, Donaldson, & Campbell, 2011, for related discussion). The effectiveness of such translation is a matter of construct validity in the Shadish et al. (2002) formulation. But it has considerable import for generalizability. If a given way of implementing the program is effective in modifying the core intended mediator in some contexts but not others, then the program effect will vary accordingly.

Developing Models of Programs' Affordance of Generalizability

Another potentially fruitful direction involves the development and testing of models of different types of programs/program circumstances in relation to the expected generalizability of effects. Different types of radioactive materials vary in the length of their half-life. Similarly, different types of programs/program circumstance are likely to vary in terms of Cronbach's "half-life of generalizations." We might be able to describe alternative types of programs and circumstances, with some expected to be more robust and others more frail with respect to generalization.

Consider two kinds of programs for which generalization is likely to be limited in scope and time. As Pawson (2006) pointed out, for certain programs there are competing or countervailing forces acting against the persistence of effects over time. As an example, anticrime interventions (such as closed-caption TV, or CCTV, and police foot patrols) are likely to have only local and transitory effects. Criminals tend not to give up, but move to another neighborhood, or learn how to circumvent or otherwise foil the intervention (e.g., by disabling CCTV). When such competing or countervailing forces are expected, efforts to generalize effects over time are likely to be tenuous. A relatively short "half-life of generalization" is also to be expected for programs that are moderated by numerous unknown moderators. When many factors matter greatly for program effectiveness but are not known, and when these factors vary across time and setting, efforts to generalize are not likely to succeed.

In contrast, there may be types of interventions for which the half-life of generalizations may be longer. For instance, there has of late been interest in the application of a classic phenomenon in the learning literature, massed versus distributed practice. This old research literature examined the relative amount of learning and retention, given a fixed amount of practice that was either done in one chunk (massed) or spread out over multiple occasions (distributed). It is too early to tell, but the application of massed versus distributed practice in math instruction might depend on rather common and general cognitive processes and thus may be fairly robust, relative to the effects of CCTV.

Of course, attempts to classify programs and contexts in terms of the challenges to generalizability will themselves have limits (as illustrated by the development of resistance to what were once thought to be robust antibiotics). Nevertheless, better thinking and practice may be a result.

Combining Confirmatory and Exploratory Analyses

Another potential direction involves using a better mix of exploratory and confirmatory analyses, especially in more quantitatively oriented outcome evaluations. Evaluations that draw on quasi-experimental and experimental design generally test an a priori hypothesis. In many (if not most) cases, the initial hypothesis is general, involving only the average treatment–comparison group contrast, or at best consideration of a few potential moderators. Well-known prohibitions against fishing act against repeated slicing and dicing of the data, to reduce well-founded concerns about significant findings arising by chance. But this does not allow evaluators to learn more about unexpected contingencies whereby the program has different effects for different types of clients or in different contexts—knowledge that could greatly contribute to appropriate generalization.

One approach, in need of further development and technical refinement, can be called "principled discovery" (Mark, 2003; Mark et al., 2011). In this approach, the evaluator still carries out planned analyses to test an a priori hypothesis (e.g., that a new STEM program will lead to better outcomes than treatment as usual). In addition, principled discovery includes two other phases (possibly with further iteration between the two).

In the first phase, the researcher would carry out exploratory analyses. For example, the STEM evaluator might examine whether the program has differential effects by looking sequentially for interaction effects with variables on which participants have been measured (e.g., gender, race, age, parental education, and so forth). Such exploration includes risks, especially the possibility of being misled by chance. Statistical significance means that a given finding is unlikely to have arisen by chance if there really were no difference. But conducting multiple exploratory tests, without an adjustment, magnifies the risk of results that are significant because of chance. Stigler's (1987, p. 148) admonition is apt: "Beware of testing too many hypotheses; the more you torture the data, the more likely they are to confess, but confession obtained under duress may not be admissible . . ."

If the exploratory analyses provide an interesting discovery, the classic admonition is to seek replication of the discovery in another study. However, this will often (but not inevitably) be infeasible in program evaluations. Thus the second phase of principled discovery would be called for, with the researcher seeking one or another form of independent (or quasi-independent) confirmation of the discovery. In many instances, this will involve other tests that can be carried out within the same data set (although data might be drawn from other data sets, or new data might be collected after phase one). For example, if an interaction were observed such that the STEM program has a smaller effect for children in families with lower parental education, this could lead to another prediction: A similar, probably stronger interaction will be obtained with a composite variable drawn from home visits, based on the amount of children's books and educational material in the home. The value of the phase 2 test is that, if the original discovery is not real but instead is due only to chance, then there is generally little if any reason to expect the phase 2 test to be confirmed.

Principled discovery holds some degree of promise in helping increase the ability of evaluations to guide future action. Potentially it can help identify moderated relationships that constrain generalizations from outcome evaluation findings that report an overall treatment effect. Future application of the approach, including further investigation of techniques for controlling for error rate in the two phases of principled discovery, seems warranted.

Highlighting Ways to Integrate Multiple Forms of Evidence and Reasoning in Support of Generalizability

Cronbach (1982, p. 70) wrote that it takes "many strands of evidence and reasoning" to support a generalization beyond the specific persons, settings, and times observed in an evaluation. However, one can readily find instances of evaluation practice that do not take this advice seriously. To support a defensible inference about generalizability, evidence beyond the evaluation findings may be needed. For example, what is known about the kinds of participants and settings to which the findings are to be applied? What do other evaluations and the relevant literature tell us about variations in responses to comparable programs (or other conceptually similar changes)? Knowing the desired target of generalizability, what are the caveats about which would-be generalizers should be aware?

More generally, it might be possible to identify models and exemplars of weaving together "many strands of reasoning and evidence" in support of generalizing—and the setting of appropriate limits on generalizing. Future directions in generalizability might profitably include improved integration of other findings and theory with evaluation findings, as well as integrate one or more of the other suggestions made in this chapter.

References

Campbell, D. T. (1984). Can we be scientific in applied social science? In R. F. Conner, D. G. Altman, & C. Jackson (Eds.), *Evaluation studies review annual* (Vol. 9, pp. 26–48). Beverly Hills, CA: Sage.

Campbell, D. T., & Stanley, J. C. (1963). Experimental and quasi-experimental designs for research on teaching. In N. L. Gage (Ed.), *Handbook of research on teaching* (pp. 171–246). Chicago, IL: Rand McNally. Also published as Campbell, D. T., & Stanley, J. C. (1966). *Experimental and quasi-experimental designs for research.* Chicago, IL: Rand McNally. Since reprinted as Campbell, D. T., & Stanley, J. (1963). *Experimental and quasi-experimental designs for research.* Boston, MA: Houghton-Mifflin/Wadsworth.

Chen, H. T. (2005). *Practical program evaluation: Assessing and improving planning, implementation, and effectiveness.* Thousand Oaks, CA: Sage.

Chen, H. T. (2010). The bottom-up approach to integrative validity: A new perspective for program evaluation. *Evaluation and Program Planning, 33,* 205–214.

Cook, T. D. (1990). The generalization of causal connections: Multiple theories in search of clear practice. In L. Sechrest, E. Perrin, & J. Bunker (Eds.), *Research methodology: Strengthening causal interpretations of nonexperimental data* (DHHS Publication No. PHS 90–3454, pp. 9–31). Rockville, MD: Department of Health and Human Services.

Cook, T. D., & Campbell, D. T. (1979). *Quasi-experimentation: Design and analysis issues for field settings.* Chicago: Rand McNally.

Cronbach, L. J. (1982). *Designing evaluations of educational and social programs.* San Francisco: Jossey-Bass.

Donaldson, S. I. (2007). *Program theory-driven evaluation science: Strategies and applications.* New York: Routledge.

Guba, F. G., & Lincoln, Y. S. (1989). *Fourth generation evaluation.* Newbury Park, CA: Sage.

House, E. R. (2002). Unfinished business: Causes and values. *American Journal of Evaluation, 22*(3), 309–315.

Mark, M. M. (1986). Validity typologies and the logic and practice of quasi-experimentation. In W. M. K. Trochim (Ed.), *Advances in quasi-experimental design and analysis* (pp. 47–66). San Francisco: Jossey-Bass.

Mark, M. M. (2003). Program evaluation. In S. A. Schinka & W. Velicer (Eds.), *Comprehensive handbook of psychology* (Vol. 2, pp. 323–347). New York: Wiley.

Mark, M. M., Donaldson, S., & Campbell, B. (2011). *Social psychology and evaluation.* New York: Guilford.

Maxwell, J. A. (1992). Understanding and validity in qualitative research. *Harvard Educational Review, 62*(3), 279–300.

Patton, M. Q. (2008) *Utilization-focused evaluation* (4th ed.). Thousand Oaks, CA: Sage.

Pawson, R. (2006). Simple principles for the evaluation of complex programmes. In A. Killoran et al. (Eds.), *Evidence based public health.* New York: Oxford University Press.

Reichardt, C. S. (2006). The principle of parallelism in the design of studies to estimate treatment effects. *Psychological Methods, 11,* 1–18.

Shadish, W. R., Cook, T. D., & Campbell, D. T. (2002). *Experimental and quasi-experimental designs for generalized causal inference.* Boston, MA: Houghton Mifflin.

Stake, R. E. (1978). The case study method in social inquiry. *Educational Researcher,* 7(2), 5–8.

Stake, R. E. (2004a). Stake and responsive evaluation. *Evaluation roots: Tracing theorists' views and influences.* Thousand Oaks, CA: Sage.

Stake, R. E. (2004b). *Standards-based and responsive evaluation.* Thousand Oaks, CA: Sage.

Stigler, S. M. (1987). Testing hypotheses or fitting models: Another look at mass extinction. In M. H. Nitecki & A. Hoffman (Eds.), *Neutral models in biology* (pp. 145–149). Oxford, United Kingdom: Oxford University Press.

MELVIN M. MARK is professor and head of psychology at Penn State University.

Reichardt, C. S. (2011). Criticisms of and an alternative to the Shadish, Cook, and Campbell validity typology. In H. T. Chen, S. I. Donaldson, & M. M. Mark (Eds.), *Advancing validity in outcome evaluation: Theory and practice. New Directions for Evaluation, 130,* 43–53.

4

Criticisms of and an Alternative to the Shadish, Cook, and Campbell Validity Typology

Charles S. Reichardt

Abstract

I give four criticisms of the Shadish, Cook, and Campbell (2002) typology of validity. An alternative typology is proposed that avoids these criticisms. © Wiley Periodicals, Inc., and the American Evaluation Association.

The distinction between internal and external validity was introduced by Campbell (1957) and subsequently immortalized in Campbell and Stanley's (1966) seminal treatise on quasi-experimentation. Cook and Campbell (1979) revised Campbell and Stanley, and added construct validity and statistical conclusion validity to turn the original bipartite categorization of validity into its current fourfold version. In the latest reincarnation, Shadish, Cook, and Campbell (SCC; 2002) updated and further refined the fourfold typology. The present chapter describes four criticisms of the SCC typology and proposes an alternative conceptualization that avoids them.

Thanks to Nicole Cundiff, Nathaniel Jungbluth, Gary Henry, Mel Mark, Georg Matt, Will Shadish, and Steve West for helpful comments on prior drafts.

NEW DIRECTIONS FOR EVALUATION, no. 130, Summer 2011 © Wiley Periodicals, Inc., and the American Evaluation Association. Published online in Wiley Online Library (wileyonlinelibrary.com) • DOI: 10.1002/ev.364

The Context for Evaluating Validity

Validity means truth. As SCC (p. 34) explain: "We use the term *validity* to refer to the approximate truth of an inference. When we say something is valid, we make a judgment about the extent to which relevant evidence supports that inference as being true or correct."

Because validity means truth, validity is an attribute of an inference. As SCC (p. 34) note: "Validity is a property of inferences. It is *not* a property of designs or methods, for the same design may contribute to more or less valid inferences under different circumstances." Because validity is a property of an inference and because SCC's validity typology focuses on causal inference, the proper context for evaluating SCC's typology is causal inference.

Criticism 1: Redundancy Between Construct and External Validity

SCC present construct and external validity as separate types of validity. But in the context of causal inference, construct and external validity are equivalent, as I explain next.

SCC use the label "sampling particulars" to refer to the specific treatments, outcomes, settings, and persons in a given study. In the SCC (p. 38) typology, construct validity concerns the truth of "inferences about the higher order constructs that represent sampling particulars." For example, SCC (p. 94) note, "A challenge to construct validity might be that we have mischaracterized the settings in a health care study as private sector hospitals and that it would have been more accurate to call them private nonprofit hospitals to distinguish them from the for-profit hospitals that were not in the study." Following the same logic, innumerable other challenges to construct validity are possible. Perhaps none of the hospitals in the study have a female CEO, so it might also be more accurate to describe the settings as private nonprofit hospitals with male CEOs. Or perhaps none of the hospitals in the study have a CEO younger than 48 or older than 59, so it might be more accurate to describe the settings as private nonprofit hospitals with male CEOs older than 47 but younger than 60. Or perhaps all the hospitals in the study have unionized janitorial staffs, so it might be more accurate to add that restriction as well. Such challenges to construct validity could continue ad infinitum. How does a researcher know where to stop? How does a researcher know which challenges to construct validity must be accepted and which may be denied?

The answer is the following. That a higher-order construct represents the sampling particulars in the context of a causal inference implies that, if a higher-order construct were substituted in place of the sampling particulars in that causal inference, the inference would remain valid. For example, if the sample contains only hospitals with male CEOs and if the causal inference a researcher is making would not hold true across hospitals with both male and female CEOs, the higher-order construct must be restricted to hospitals with male CEOs for that causal inference. On the other hand,

NEW DIRECTIONS FOR EVALUATION • DOI: 10.1002/ev

if the causal inference a researcher is drawing would hold true across hospitals with either male or female CEOs, then the higher-order construct need not be restricted to hospitals with male CEOs for that causal inference. So whether sampling particulars are validly represented by a higher-order construct depends necessarily on the context in which the higher-order construct is used. And, as shown above, in the context of a causal inference, whether a higher-order construct accurately represents the sampling particulars of a study's settings (such as types of hospitals) depends on how the causal relationship in that causal inference varies across the different types of settings (e.g., whether the causal relationship does or does not hold across CEO gender). More generally, in the context of a causal inference, whether a higher-order construct accurately represents the sampling particulars of participants, treatments, outcomes, and settings depends on how the causal relationship in that causal inference varies across different types of participants, treatments, outcomes, and settings. When a higher-order construct is to be used in a causal inference, there is simply no other way to determine which challenges to construct validity must be accepted and which may be denied.

The conclusion to be drawn is that, in the context of causal inference, assessing construct validity is equivalent to determining whether the causal relationship under study holds over variations in persons, settings, treatment, or outcomes. But that is how SCC (p. 38) define external validity, which is "the validity of inferences about whether the cause–effect relationship holds over variation in persons, settings, treatment variables, and measurement variables." In other words, whether a higher-order construct represents the sampling particulars in a study (which is the question of construct validity) is determined by how the causal relationship under study holds across variations in people, settings, treatment, or outcomes (which is the question of external validity). For example, whether the higher-order construct used to describe the hospitals in a study must include reference to the gender of the CEOs (which is a question of construct validity) depends on how the causal relationship under study varies across the gender of the CEO (which is a question of external validity). In spite of SCC's specification that construct and external validity address different questions, in the context of causal inference, construct and external validity ask the same questions.

The equivalence of external and construct validity is also revealed by comparing the threats to external validity to the threats to construct validity. First, note that the threats to construct validity listed in SCC (p. 73) are specific construct errors, whereas the threats to external validity listed in SCC (p. 87) are described as generic interactions. Then note that the specific errors that SCC list under construct validity are simply instances of the generic interactions that SCC list under external validity. For example, the threat to construct validity called "reactivity to the experimental situation" (which arises when the effect of a treatment varies with the reactivity of the

NEW DIRECTIONS FOR EVALUATION • DOI: 10.1002/ev

research setting) is an instance of the threat to external validity called "inter-actions of the causal relationship with settings." Similarly, the threat to construct validity called "treatment diffusion" (which arises when the size of a treatment effect varies because of the diffusion of the treatment) is an instance of the threat to external validity called "interactions of the causal relationship over treatment variations." And the threat to construct validity called "treatment sensitive factorial structure" (which arises when the treatment effect varies with the structure of the outcome measurement) is an instance of the threat to external validity called "interactions of the causal relationship with outcomes."

Construct and external validity are not redundant in the validity typology in Cook and Campbell (1979) because Cook and Campbell give construct and external validity nonoverlapping sets of referents. Cook and Campbell define construct validity as applying only to generalizations about the putative cause and the effect in a study, whereas external validity is restricted to generalizations about people, settings, and times. SCC expand the definitions of construct and external validity so that each applies to treatments, outcomes, people, and settings. By making the referents for construct and external validity the same, SCC also make construct and external validity equivalent, in the context of causal inference.

Construct validity subsumes external validity. External validity is defined only with reference to causal inferences, whereas construct validity is defined more broadly because it holds in noncausal contexts as well. In the only context in which external validity is defined (which is the context of causal inference), external and construct validity are equivalent. Rather than having four distinct criteria for evaluating the validity of casual inference as claimed, SCC have only three.

Criticism 2: The Meaning of External Validity

External validity, as made clear by its name, is a type of validity. Because all types of validity concern the truth of inferences (SCC, p. 34), external validity must, by definition, also concern the truth of inferences. In particular, external validity concerns the truth of generalizations about causal relationships, regardless of the breadth or narrowness of those generalizations. That is, as long as a generalization about a causal relationship is true, it is externally valid even if the generalization is exceedingly narrow. SCC could not define external validity in any other way because validity refers to truth and truth alone. Unfortunately, many, if not most, researchers interpret external validity to mean something different. Many, if not most, researchers believe external validity refers not just to the truth of generalizations but also to their breadth. The importance of this distinction is explained next.

Consider an example. Suppose the participants in a study are volunteers and the results of the study hold only for volunteers. If a researcher correctly draws the conclusion that the causal relationship in the study holds only for volunteers (which means the researcher does not generalize the results to nonvolunteers), that conclusion is externally valid, as defined by SCC. In contrast, both researchers and textbook authors (e.g., Goodwin, 2008) often state an inference lacks external validity if it cannot be generalized to a broader set of participants than just volunteers. In particular, because the results in the preceding example do not generalize to nonvolunteers whose behavior is likely to be of greater interest than that of volunteers, researchers would say the results lack external validity. But this is an incorrect application of external validity according to SCC's definition (as well as to the Cook and Campbell, 1979, definition).

Or consider the well-known article by Mook (1983) entitled "In defense of external invalidity." According to SCC's definition of external validity (wherein a causal inference is externally valid if it contains a correct generalization of a cause–effect relationship), defending external *invalidity*, as Mook does, would mean defending generalizations that are untrue, which would be ridiculous if it were what Mook intends. But it is not. Mook's defense of external invalidity is a defense not of untrue statements, but of statements that do not generalize broadly which, as he shows, can be defensible in many circumstances. In other words, the only reason it makes sense to defend external invalidity, as Mook does, is that Mook's use of external validity differs from SCC's. That Mook's article passed peer review and has been widely cited suggests that Mook's (mis)interpretation of external validity is widely accepted.

Disagreement about the interpretation of external validity has also caused confusion, I believe, in disputes such as that between Cronbach (1982) and Cook and Campbell (1979) over the relative priority of internal and external validity. To Cook and Campbell, internal validity takes priority over external validity because external validity asks if a causal relationship (which has been found to exist based on an assessment of internal validity) has been generalized correctly. Such a priority ordering is justified because it makes no sense to ask if a causal relationship has been generalized correctly, unless one first knows that the causal relationship exists (which is the question of internal validity). In contrast, Cronbach believes external validity takes priority over internal validity because he believes external validity asks whether the causal relationship under study answers the question about cause that one wants answered (i.e., whether the results found in the study can be generalized broadly enough to apply to the populations of greatest interest). Such a priority ordering is justified because it makes no sense to devote resources to determining whether a causal relationship exists (which is the question of internal validity) unless that relationship can be used to answer the question that one wants answered (which is the question of external validity, according to Cronbach). The dispute would rest on firmer ground if the disputants were not using different definitions of external validity.

Perhaps the SCC typology should not be faulted because others misinterpret it. But the misinterpretation is rampant. And the misinterpretation arises because questions about the breadth, and not just the truth, of an inference are critical in both basic and applied research. A complete typology of criticisms of inferences should include the criticism that an inference is too narrow and not just that it is invalid. A defender of SCC might argue that the SCC typology is meant to explicate validity and not other criticisms. But that is exactly the problem. The SCC typology emphasizes validity to the exclusion of other equally important criteria. That researchers have reinterpreted external validity to serve another purpose suggests just how important that other purpose is. As indicated by its title, the SCC volume is focused on causal generalization. Given this focus, it is just as important to ask whether generalizations are too narrow as whether generalizations are correct.

Criticism 3: Conflating Validity and Precision

Validity and precision are orthogonal. The statement "It may rain tomorrow" conveys no information and hence is imprecise, but it is true, and hence valid. Conversely, the claim "It will rain in Denver tomorrow at 2:00 p.m." makes a very precise prediction but may well be wrong, and hence invalid. The same independence between validity and precision holds when estimating treatment effects. An estimate of a treatment effect is precise if the estimate's confidence interval is narrow. A statement containing an estimate of the size of a treatment effect could be valid, and yet the treatment effect could be estimated imprecisely (i.e., with a wide confidence interval). Conversely, a statement about the size of a treatment effect could be invalid and yet the treatment effect could be estimated (incorrectly) with great precision (i.e., with a narrow confidence interval). A valid confidence interval can be either wide or narrow. The same holds for an invalid confidence interval. Researchers drawing causal inferences should be careful to make the distinction between validity and precision lest they overlook one in favor of the other (Reichardt & Gollob, 1987). Rather than drawing a clear distinction between validity and precision, SCC conflate the two, as do Cook and Campbell (1979). For example, factors that affect the precision of estimates are listed incorrectly in SCC as threats to statistical conclusion *validity*, as explained next.

As defined by SCC, a threat to statistical conclusion validity can arise when researchers use either statistical significance tests or confidence intervals. For an inference involving a confidence interval, it is easy to see that several of the threats to statistical conclusion validity listed in SCC are not threats to validity, but to precision. For example, the threats to validity of "heterogeneity of units" and "extraneous variance in the experimental setting" increase the width of a confidence interval, which makes the treatment-effect estimate imprecise, but does not make the confidence interval incorrect or invalid.

That SCC include threats to precision among their list of threats to validity can also be seen from the perspective of statistical significance tests. Several of the threats to statistical conclusion validity that SCC list (including "low statistical power," "heterogeneity of units," and "extraneous variance in the experimental setting") can, as SCC note, lead to Type II errors when statistical significance tests are used. But Type II errors are errors of imprecision and not errors of invalidity. A Type II error arises when the null hypothesis is false but the results of a hypothesis test do not reach statistical significance. Under these circumstances, the conclusion that should be drawn is that the null hypothesis cannot be rejected. Such a conclusion conveys little information, and so is imprecise. But it is a conclusion that is true, and hence valid. Therefore, as long as the results of the statistical significance test are interpreted properly, a Type II error is not an invalid inference and so is not a threat to validity.

Of course, researchers sometimes interpret Type II errors improperly. In particular, in the presence of a Type II error, researchers sometimes make the mistake of accepting the null hypothesis rather than concluding, as they should, that the null hypothesis cannot be rejected. Accepting the null hypothesis is likely to be an incorrect conclusion and hence invalid. But such a mistake is not a fault of low statistical power—it is a mistake in the interpretation of the results of a statistical significance test, regardless of the level of power. If the source of such an inferential error were labeled correctly, it would be called the threat to validity due to "accepting the null hypothesis" (and SCC should, but do not, include such a threat in their extensive lists). But a Type II error need not (and, indeed, should not) lead researchers to accept the null hypothesis. Accepting the null hypothesis, and not low statistical power per se, is the source of invalidity when a Type II error leads to a false conclusion. Because low statistical power makes an inference imprecise but does not make it invalid, it is a mistake for SCC to characterize sources of low statistical power as threats to validity.

It may be difficult to appreciate the distinction being drawn above between Type II errors and accepting the null hypothesis. So it may be difficult to appreciate how the SCC typology conflates precision with validity. The critical point is that precision and validity are independent, so it is impossible for SCC to address properly the issue of precision under the rubric of validity. To the extent the SCC typology addresses the problem of imprecision under the rubric of statistical conclusion validity, SCC mischaracterize the problem of imprecision. But to the extent the SCC typology of validity does not address the problem of imprecision well, it omits reference to a central concern in statistical inference. At best, the SCC typology incorrectly conflates precision and validity. At worst, the SCC typology overlooks precision.

Criticism 4: Omitting Time

Cook and Campbell (1979) include generalizations about time as part of external validity. For example, Cook and Campbell (1979, p. 39) define external validity as concerned with "the generalizability of a causal relationship to and across populations of persons, settings, and times." In contrast, SCC do not include generalization across times in their definition of external validity. That is, SCC (p. 38) define external validity as "the validity of inferences about whether the cause–effect relationship holds over variation in persons, settings, treatment variables, and measurement variables" with "times" conspicuously missing. In addition, SCC's (p. 87) list of threats to external validity includes interactions of the causal relationship with people, settings, treatment variables, and outcome variables, but not with times. Similarly, SCC (p. 39) define construct validity as asking "which general constructs are involved in the persons, settings, treatments and observations used in the experiment," again with "times" excluded. SCC (p. 54) do explicitly include "times" (along with treatments, outcomes, settings, and persons) as sampling particulars that are involved in internal validity. But, although it is possible for time to be confounded with the treatment (see Reichardt, 2006), no such confound is listed as a threat to either internal or construct validity in SCC.

Time is sometimes intentionally overlooked in making generalizations because time is thought to be subsumed under the rubric of settings. However, time refers not only to the chronological time in which results are embedded, but also to the time lag between the implementation of a treatment and the assessment of its effects, which is distinguishable from the setting. Because effects can vary dramatically over different time lags independently of the setting, time lag should be of central and independent concern in making causal inferences and drawing generalizations (Gollob & Reichardt, 1987). For example, the sleeper effect (Cook, Gruder, Hennigan, & Flay, 1979) provides a compelling illustration of the importance of time lags in causal relationships.

Like SCC, Cronbach (1982) omitted time from his validity typology because he believed time was subsumed by other features of his formulation. But Reichardt's (2006) principle of parallelism explains why a theory of causality should place time on equal footing with people, settings, treatments, and outcome variables. Time (including time lag) is overlooked in the definitions of external and construct validity and in the lists of threats to validity in SCC (although not excluded from frequent mention elsewhere in the volume).

An Alternative Typology

A comprehensive theory of causal inference should emphasize the most important criteria for evaluating causal inferences. High on the list of evaluative criteria should be validity, precision, and generalizability.

The Criterion of Validity

The size of a treatment effect depends on the nature of the treatment as well as on the four factors of the recipients, settings, times, and outcome variables

(Reichardt, 2006). The recipients are the entities that receive the treatment and upon which outcomes are measured. The settings are the environments in which the treatment is implemented and outcomes are assessed. Times refer to two chronological points in time: the time at which the treatment is implemented and the time at which outcome variables are assessed. Hence time includes reference to the time lag between these two time points. The outcome variables refer to the measurements on which outcomes are assessed. Because the size of an effect can vary with the treatments, recipients, settings, times, and outcome variables, these five factors are called size-of-effect factors. Conceptually, the size-of-effect factors are the who (recipients), what (outcome variables), where (settings), when (times), and how (treatments) of an effect. An effect is labeled by specifying the five size-of-effect factors.

An estimate of an effect is invalid if the estimate doesn't match the label it is given. For example, a researcher might label an estimate as equal to the effect of a treatment when the estimate really equals the effect of the treatment plus the effects of selection differences. Or, for another example, the recipients could be incorrectly labeled private hospitals when they should have been labeled private nonprofit hospitals. The label for an estimate can be mismatched on any of the five size-of-effect factors. That is, the treatments can be mislabeled, or the recipients can be mislabeled, or the settings can be mislabeled, or the times can be mislabeled, or the outcome variables can be mislabeled. A more complete explication of validity is given in Reichardt (2006).

The Criterion of Precision

In most cases, the size of an effect can be estimated with confidence only within a range of values. The precision of an estimate concerns the width of the range of values for a given level of confidence. The criticism that an estimate is imprecise is independent of the criticism of invalidity. For example, the statement that the size of an effect falls between negative infinity and positive infinity with 100% confidence is valid, but too imprecise for any meaningful purpose. Conversely, the statement that the size of an effect is equal to a single number with 100% confidence is highly precise, but likely to be invalid. In other words, a confidence interval can be correctly labeled (and hence valid), while at the same time imprecise, or vice versa.

An estimate can be imprecise because of heterogeneity or extraneous variability in the samples of treatments, recipients, settings, times, or outcomes variables. That is, the criterion of precision is relevant to each of the five size-of-effect factors. Precision is an important evaluative criterion because a highly imprecise estimate, even if valid, is of little use.

The Criterion of Generalizability

An effect is generalizable to the extent it varies relatively little across a given range of treatments, recipients, settings, times, or outcome variables.

NEW DIRECTIONS FOR EVALUATION • DOI: 10.1002/ev

Generalizability applies to all five size-of-effect factors and an effect can be differentially generalizable across treatments, recipients, settings, times, or outcome variables.

As explained above, many researchers mistakenly believe that external validity concerns generalizability, as defined here. But in the alternative typology, validity and generalizability are distinct. A validly labeled estimate can be either widely or narrowly generalizable.

Generalizability is important because the combination of treatments, recipients, settings, times, and outcome variables contained in a study will never be the same in future implementations. Therefore, knowledge of generalizability is required if evaluators or policy makers are to predict the effects that would arise were a program to be disseminated.

Comparison With the SCC Typology

By distinguishing among the three evaluative criteria, the alternative typology proposed here avoids several of the weaknesses in the SCC typology. Unlike the SSC typology, in the alternative typology, the three evaluative criteria are crossed with the five size-of-effect factors. That is, in accordance with the principle of parallelism (Reichardt, 2006), each of the three evaluative criteria applies to each of the five size-of-effect factors. As they are defined in SCC, the categories of statistical conclusion and internal, construct, and external validity are not emphasized in the alternative typology. Instead, the alternative conceptualization emphasizes both the underlying commonality of all threats to validity (namely, that all threats to validity are mismatches between a label and an estimate of an effect) and that threats to validity apply in a parallel fashion across all five size-of-effect factors. At the same time, all the threats to validity in SCC (plus ones overlooked in SCC) are included in the alternative typology. Also unlike the SCC typology, where the focus of attention is sometimes restricted to inferences about the existence of effects, the alternative typology focuses explicitly on inferences about the size of effects, which encompasses inferences about the existence of effects as a special case. Further details are provided in Reichardt (2006).

Conclusion

The three criteria of validity, precision, and generalizability for evaluating causal inferences are distinct and should neither be overlooked nor conflated. In evaluating a causal inference, researchers should consider how each of these three evaluative criteria applies to each of the five size-of-effect factors of treatments, recipients, settings, times, and outcome variables.

The SCC typology does not adequately distinguish validity from precision and generalizability. The typology in SCC does not well address the three evaluative criteria as they apply to each of the five size-of-effect factors. The SCC typology does not adequately focus on time and time lags.

The SCC typology makes construct and external validity redundant in the context of causal inference. Most researchers believe external validity raises the question of generalizability, as defined here. But it does not. In a study of the effects of a treatment using volunteers, causal inferences about the effects of the treatment on volunteers would receive high marks on all four of SCC's validity types, including external validity, as long as the inferences that were drawn were correct. But the inferences would receive low marks on generalizability if the inference could not be applied to nonvolunteers, and that was the population of greatest interest. Researchers and policy makers need to ask not only whether inferences are valid but whether inferences are precise and whether they answer the policy questions that most need to be addressed. SCC focus too much on validity and not enough on other criteria that are equally important.

References

Campbell, D. T. (1957). Factors relevant to the validity of experiments in social settings. *Psychological Bulletin, 54*, 297–312.

Campbell, D. T., & Stanley, J. C. (1966). *Experimental and quasi-experimental designs for research.* Chicago: Rand McNally.

Cook, T. D., & Campbell, D. T. (1979). *Quasi-experimentation: Design and analysis issues for field settings.* Chicago: Rand McNally.

Cook, T. D., Gruder, C. L., Hennigan, K. M., & Flay, B. R. (1979). History of the sleeper effect: Some logical pitfalls in accepting the null hypothesis. *Psychological Bulletin, 86*, 662–679.

Cronbach, L. J. (1982). *Designing evaluations of educational and social programs.* San Francisco, CA: Jossey-Bass.

Gollob, H. F., & Reichardt, C. S. (1987). Taking account of time lags in causal models. *Child Development, 58*, 80–92.

Goodwin, G. J. (2008). *Research in psychology: Methods and design* (5th ed.). New York: Wiley.

Mook, D. G. (1983). In defense of external invalidity. *American Psychologist, 38*, 379–387.

Reichardt, C. S. (2006). The principle of parallelism in the design of studies to estimate treatment effects. *Psychological Methods, 11*, 1–18.

Reichardt, C. S., & Gollob, H. F. (1987). Taking uncertainty into account when estimating effects. In M. M. Mark & R. L. Shotland (Eds.), *Multiple methods for program evaluation. New Directions for Program Evaluation, 35*, 7–22.

Shadish, W. R., Cook, T. D., & Campbell, D. T. (2002). *Experimental and quasi-experimental designs for generalized causal inference.* Boston, MA: Houghton Mifflin.

CHARLES S. REICHARDT is a professor of psychology at the University of Denver.

Julnes, G. (2011). Reframing validity in research and evaluation: A multidimensional, systematic model of valid inference. In H. T. Chen, S. I. Donaldson, & M. M. Mark (Eds.), *Advancing validity in outcome evaluation: Theory and practice. New Directions for Evaluation, 130,* 55–67.

5

Reframing Validity in Research and Evaluation: A Multidimensional, Systematic Model of Valid Inference

George Julnes

Abstract

The importance of promoting valid conclusions from causal inquiry has animated efforts to be more systematic in our conceptions of validity. This chapter elaborates on the systematization of Shadish, Cook, and Campbell (2002) to offer a multidimensional framework of validity that is more comprehensive, more applicable to qualitative inquiry, and more flexible in guiding the progression of our understanding in specific contexts. © Wiley Periodicals, Inc., and the American Evaluation Association.

Evaluation, and social science more generally, presumes that we can reach what we refer to as valid conclusions based on available evidence. Shadish, Cook, and Campbell (2002, p. 513) define validity in their glossary as "[t]he truth of, correctness of, or degree of support for an inference." Although evaluation makes use of three kinds of inference—descriptive, causal, and valuative—the emphasis in this issue on impact evaluation will lead us to focus on the first two of these three. Examples of impact claims (often stated with confidence intervals) include statements that a drug reduces the likelihood of heart attacks by 30% or that a policy change has a greater impact on the employment of men than of women.

NEW DIRECTIONS FOR EVALUATION, no. 130, Summer 2011 © Wiley Periodicals, Inc., and the American Evaluation Association. Published online in Wiley Online Library (wileyonlinelibrary.com) • DOI: 10.1002/ev.365

Claiming that conclusions are "valid" need not entail some ultimate truth about reality, but it seems clear that some conclusions are manifestly wrong, as would be the case if the drug just noted actually increased the risk of heart attacks. Recognizing that many factors can lead to inaccurate causal conclusions in research settings, people like Lee Cronbach and Donald Campbell and his colleagues developed validity frameworks to alert us to these potential sources of invalid conclusions and to suggest design solutions that, applied proactively or sometimes even post hoc, can counter those threats of error.

The most developed and accepted current validity framework is presented in Shadish, Cook, and Campbell (2002) (hereafter, SCC). Despite its obvious strengths, recent controversies, such as the debates over federal policies promoting random-assignment experimental designs (see Julnes & Rog, 2007), have led some to criticize the SCC framework. These issues were addressed in a 2008 panel for the American Evaluation Association (AEA) conference, "Revisiting Validity: Implications for Theory, Practice, and Policy," in which Ernie House (2008) presented his concerns about deliberate bias in otherwise "rigorous" pharmaceutical studies, Chip Reichardt (2008) presented his critique of the conceptual organization of the SCC framework, and I (Julnes, 2008) presented the reframing of validity frameworks summarized in this chapter.

My goal in organizing the AEA panel and for this chapter reflects my view that the SCC framework is a profound achievement and that, nonetheless, all frameworks can potentially benefit from efforts by others to offer alternative formulations. Not all offerings of this sort will be good, but, in line with Campbell's Experimenting Society, experience teaches us that though most innovations are failures, the ultimate failure is the failure to innovate. Accordingly, this chapter begins with an overview of the logic of the Campbellian framework and then suggests that the SCC framework would offer better coverage of threats to valid inference and increased conceptual clarity by reframing validity in terms of multiple intersecting factors rather than as a categorical system comprised of the standard four types—statistical conclusion, internal, construct, and external validity (Julnes, 2004).

Logic of Valid Inference in the Campbellian Framework

Campbell and colleagues developed their typology of validity in stages (Campbell, 1986; Shadish, Cook, & Leviton, 1991), beginning with internal and external validity as applied to education research (Campbell & Stanley, 1963), then adding statistical conclusion and construct validity (Cook & Campbell, 1979), and more recently reorganizing and redefining the four types of threats to valid inference (SCC). In this most recent stage, now presented as a general framework applicable to all research and evaluation, the four types are summarized in the SCC introductory sentence on the topic. "Threats to validity are specific reasons why we can be partly or completely

New Directions for Evaluation • DOI: 10.1002/ev

wrong when we make an inference about covariance, about causation, about constructs, or about whether the causal relationship holds over variations in persons, settings, treatments, and outcomes" (SCC, p. 39).

Unpacking this sentence, the SCC logic is that causal inference begins with evidence of a relationship between an intervention and an outcome. Avoiding false conclusions about the presence (or magnitude) of such a relationship is the focus of statistical conclusion validity, defined as concerning the "validity of inferences about the correlation (covariation) between treatment and outcome" (SCC, p. 38). If we are satisfied that there is a relationship, the next question, concerning internal validity, is whether this "covariation between A and B reflects a causal relationship from A to B in the form in which the variables were manipulated or measured" (p. 53). The issue here is being able to rule out the other likely causal explanations for the observed relationship (the explicated threats to internal validity).

If we judge internal validity as adequate, we move to one or both of two other judgments. One of these, referencing external validity, "concerns inferences about the extent to which a causal relationship holds over variations in persons [units], settings, treatments, and outcomes" (SCC, p. 83). The other extension, involving construct validity, concerns conclusions about what the causal relationship means, or the "validity of inferences about the higher order constructs that represent sampling particulars" (p. 38).

Thus, the logic involves a hierarchy of inferences built on confidence in a relationship (covariation) between intervention and outcomes and building on this in one or more of three ways by addressing causality, generalizability of causal relationships, and underlying constructs. With this overview, we now consider challenges to the SCC framework in the two areas of enhancing coverage of the framework and clarifying its conceptual organization.

Enhancing Coverage of Framework for Valid Inference

A validity framework is more useful as a tool to the extent that it addresses all threats to the types of valid inference important to the evaluation community. Are there categories of threats not covered in the framework? To what extent does the framework cover inferences made from different approaches, including qualitative methods? For these questions about coverage, the recommendations will be to enlarge the treatment of descriptive inferences in the SCC system and, hence, view statistical conclusion validity as a subset of the more general domain of relational validity (itself a subset of descriptive validity).

Challenges Regarding Coverage

If there are factors affecting the trustworthiness of causal inferences not included in our validity frameworks, then invalid conclusions may not be recognized as such. This, in turn, degrades the value of the framework as a guide for inquiry decisions. As SCC acknowledge, "the key to the most confident causal conclusions in our theory of validity is the ability to construct a persuasive argument that every plausible and identified threat to validity has been identified and ruled out" (SSC, p. 473).

House (2008; this issue) raises coverage issues in his critique of pharmaceutical research, where the financial interests of researchers appear to influence the research conclusions. His question is whether the reported relationships between drug treatment and positive outcomes might be deliberately manipulated because of the conflict of interests. Examples of ways that deliberate bias might manifest itself in conclusions from a study or series of studies include opportunistic choice of a comparison group, ignoring negative effects, and selective publishing. Each of these actions, and others (e.g., simply fabricating data to fit desired interpretations), can result in faulty representations of the relationship between intervention and outcomes.

In relating House's concerns to the SCC framework, recall that concerns about relationships (e.g., as represented by correlation or regression coefficients) define the domain of statistical conclusion validity. There are several subtypes of statistical conclusion validity listed in SCC (p. 45), including low statistical power, violated statistical assumptions, and even incomplete implementation of interventions, but the deliberate bias of concern to House is not in this list. Although the definition of statistical conclusion validity can be expanded to include additional factors that threaten misestimation of intervention–outcome relationships, including intentional bias threats under statistical conclusion validity would cause the category to lose much of its connection to statistics or anything quantitative.

A second challenge for coverage concerns the applicability of the SCC validity framework for qualitative inquiry. SCC acknowledges this in noting that in qualitative studies "internal validity no longer depends directly on statistical conclusion validity, though clearly an assessment that treatment covaried with the effect is still necessary" (SCC, p. 63). Combined with the gaps in coverage of threats regarding valid relationship conclusions, this lack of relevance for qualitative inquiry calls for a new approach to what statistical conclusion validity was developed to address.

Way Forward: Developing Relational Validity

Recognizing that statistical conclusion validity is too narrow a concept—not covering all relevant threats regarding relationships and not being relevant for qualitative inquiry—suggests that it is time to step back and remember the expressed intent of the Campbellian approach to focus first on valid inference regarding the nature of relationships between treatments and effects. This, as shown in Table 5.1 and of equal concern to qualitative and quantitative inquiry, is the domain of relational validity, a more general

Table 5.1. Levels of Descriptive and Causal Inference

	Descriptive Inference	Causal Inference
Observation-Based Inferences	Relational Validity Qualitative or quantitative "assessment that treatment covaried with the effect" (SCC, p. 63)	Internal Validity Causal Description: Representing the causal impact of an intervention on those affected
Inferences About Underlying Phenomena	Construct Validity Non-causal explanation of what the relationship means in construct terms	Construct Validity Causal Explanation: Providing explanations for the causal impact with construct-based accounts of how and why

domain of which statistical conclusion validity is but a part, albeit an important one.

The descriptive–causal inference distinction in Table 5.1 is fairly standard in methodology texts (King, Keohane, & Verba, 1994; Remler & Van Ryzin, 2011). The distinction between observation-based and construct-based inferences is also common, with King et al. (1994) differentiating description ("the collection of facts," p. 34) and descriptive inference, which involves "the process of understanding an unobserved phenomenon on the basis of a set of observations" (p. 55). Similarly, SCC distinguishes *causal description*, the causal inference based on observed covariation between actions and outcomes and a qualitative assessment that other causal explanations are not plausible (SCC, p. 9), and *causal explanation*, which involves inferences about unobservable causal mechanisms based on theories (often informal) of underlying dynamics.

Combining these two distinctions to define validity categories represents a shift toward a more systematic understanding of validity, a movement that SCC promotes and that we honor best by extending. As such, whereas the early groupings in the Campbellian framework were created by a pragmatic clustering of the most notable threats to validity, the SCC logic seeks to build on more fundamental distinctions. In addition to covering the validity threats that concern Ernie House as well as those of statistical conclusion validity, defining relational validity as the intersection of two distinctions has the advantage of being equally relevant for qualitative and quantitative research. It also highlights the parallel role that construct validity plays in making sense of descriptive inferences and causal inferences.

Supporting Conceptual Organization

In addition to adequate coverage, a second expectation of our validity frameworks is that they organize things in meaningful ways that have implications for effective practice. To what extent does the framework highlight dependencies such that some knowledge claims build and depend on others? To what extent does the framework group together types of conclusions that are vulnerable to the same types of threats to valid inference? Consistent with the argument above, improving the conceptual organization of validity frameworks involves moving from viewing validity in terms of four discrete types toward a more systematic view of validity as comprised of intersecting dimensions.

Challenges for Organization

The changes in definitions of validity types seen in moving from Campbell and Stanley (1963) to SCC can be understood largely as efforts to transform the framework from a loosely organized collection of useful guidance to a tightly organized conceptual scheme. The sharper conceptual distinctions that result from this movement offer advantages but also provide sharper contrasts for conceptual critiques. For example, Reichardt (this issue) claims that, unlike earlier Campbellian frameworks, the SCC framework muddles the distinction between construct and external validity so that they are, in fact, redundant. Critiques of this sort contend that the conceptual distinctions in a framework are internally inconsistent, incorrect, or at least inadequately developed. A different sort of challenge is that the SCC system does not provide useful guidance on how our different types of inferences should be viewed in relation to one another, with, for example, some (Gargani & Donaldson, this issue) rejecting internal validity as warranting primacy by virtue of being a foundation for external validity.

Way Forward: Dimensional View of Knowledge Claims

The SCC systematization of the Campbellian paradigm and the critiques that result can be understood, in part, in terms of a movement toward viewing validity claims as involving multiple, intersecting sets of distinctions rather than as the discrete categories, or "baskets," of statistical conclusion validity, internal validity, construct validity, and external validity. We can use the term *dimension* to refer to these sets of distinctions as long as we are clear not to be suggesting the definition of dimensions as continuous quantitative factors. As suggested below, this structure of intersecting dimensions is already being developed in SCC, and so our task is simply to support this ongoing development (Julnes, 2004).

Distinguishing External and Construct Validity

The move toward viewing validity as an intersection of types can be seen in the SCC treatment of external and construct validity. Campbell and Stanley (1963) did not address construct validity, whereas Cook and Campbell (1979) used construct validity to group together challenges that come from

Table 5.2. Distinguishing External and Construct Validity With Intersecting Dimensions

	Local Inference	Generalized Inference
Observation-Based Inferences	Internal Validity Causal Description: local, causal relationships	External Validity Generalized Causal Description: "sources of variation in causal relationships" (SCC, p. 468)
Inferences About Underlying Phenomena	Construct Validity Causal Explanation: "labeling research operations" in terms of underlying mechanisms (SCC, p. 468)	Construct Validity Generalized Causal Explanation: "labeling research operations" responsible for variation (SCC, p. 468)

"generalizing to causes and effects" (SCC, p. 467). This distinction, however, was less conceptual than pragmatic, dividing up some of the threats to external validity "to facilitate memory for the very long list of threats that . . . had to fit under Campbell and Stanley's umbrella conception of external validity" (p. 467). In SCC, however, the relationship between external and construct validity has been altered so that the framework now "equates construct validity with labeling research operations, and external validity with sources of variation in causal relationships" (p. 468).

Table 5.2 illustrates a way to visualize this intended contrast such that construct and external validity support each other but are not redundant. For example, beginning with internal validity in the top-left corner of Table 5.2, labeling the constructs involved in a local causal relationship can and should suggest "mechanisms" that predict how relationships will generalize. However, proper labeling "is not a necessary condition for external validity" (SCC, p. 469) because it is possible to reach valid estimates of the strength of causal relationships in other populations without an adequate understanding of underlying constructs.

Elaboration of Intersecting Dimensions of Inferences. The value of the intersecting dimensions for distinguishing internal, external, and construct validity suggests considering additional dimensions that capture the complexity of our knowledge claims. Figure 5.1 adds the two dimensions derived from Campbell's (1986) definition of internal validity as "local molar causal validity." Internal validity is *molar* in being concerned with aggregate relationships between an entire intervention package and measured outcomes. This is traditionally contrasted (SCC, p. 11) with analyses of moderated relationships (differential relationships and impacts) when analyzed across what Cronbach (1982) called UTOS: variations in Units, Treatments, Outcomes, or Settings, though one could add Reichardt's (this issue) *time*

Figure 5.1. Relationships Among Varieties of Local, Observation-Based Inference

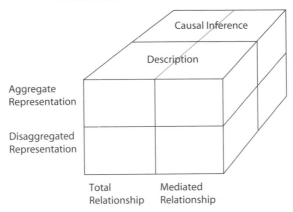

factor, as well, and of mediated relationships (sequences or causal linkages, as when an employment support program leads to increased earnings only for those who also increased their work skills during the program). Presenting Figure 5.1 in three dimensions highlights that we can elaborate our understanding along any one or more of the dimensions displayed.

Organizing Validity Types by Similarity of Threats and Responses

Combining the dimensions in Tables 5.1 and 5.2 and Figure 5.1 yields five sets of distinctions with 32 different types of inference (2 * 2 * 2 * 2 * 2 cells in the matrix). Interestingly, the traditional SCC definition of internal validity applies to only 1 of these 32 cells (local molar causal inference), which allows a certain purity of meaning but also leaves the other three types of validity in the SCC system to cover, with less purity, the remaining 31 cells. Such an imbalance suggests revisiting the framework, with one possibility being to group inference types into categories based on the threats to validity for which each type is most vulnerable. Figure 5.2 presents such an organization, with the types of validity defined as the intersections of our dimensions, though, to be manageable in a two-dimensional form, the distinctions for moderated and mediated conclusions are depicted as embedded rows rather than as the independent dimensions of Figure 5.1.

In addition to the already discussed use of relational validity to broaden the focus of statistical conclusion validity, the major change from the SCC framework presented in Figure 5.2 concerns the positioning of conclusions about mediated and moderated relationships. For example, in SCC, a conclusion that an intervention had a greater causal impact on the men studied than on women falls in the domain of external validity. In contrast, in Figure 5.2 all observation-based causal knowledge claims about what was studied (the people in the study, the conditions of the study) are in the

Figure 5.2. Systematic Framework for Valid Causal Inference

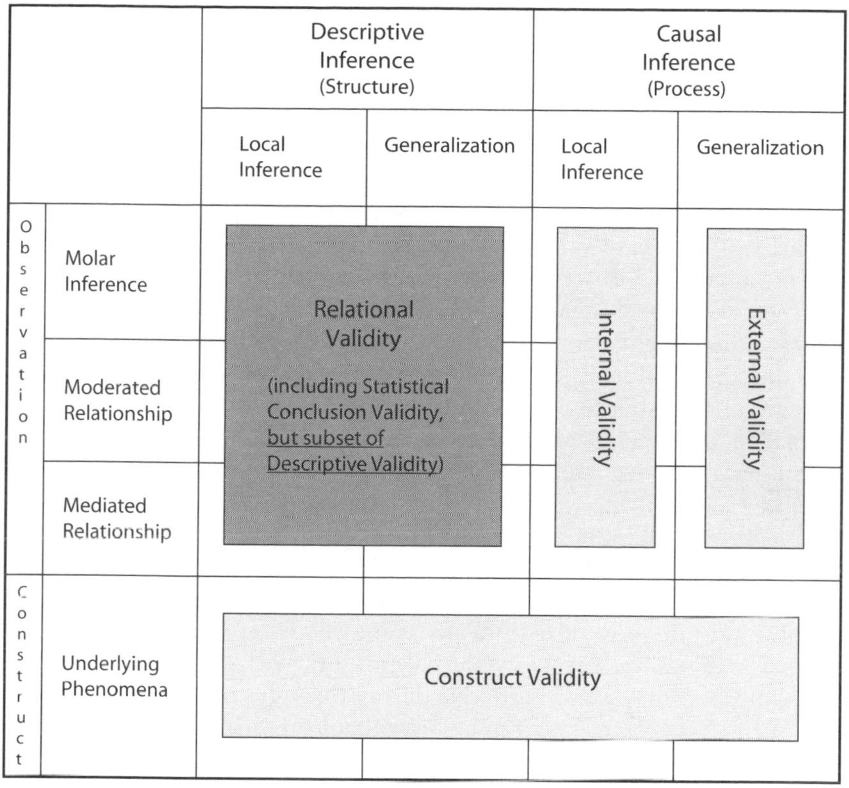

		Descriptive Inference (Structure)		Causal Inference (Process)	
		Local Inference	Generalization	Local Inference	Generalization
O b s e r v a t i o n	Molar Inference	Relational Validity (including Statistical Conclusion Validity, but subset of Descriptive Validity)		Internal Validity	External Validity
	Moderated Relationship				
	Mediated Relationship				
C o n s t r u c t	Underlying Phenomena	Construct Validity			

domain of internal validity. An advantage of this organization is that all the familiar threats to internal validity apply equally to moderated and mediated local causal claims as well—the above claim that a treatment was more effective for the men studied than for the women studied needs to be evaluated in terms of the same selection-bias threats as needed for aggregate claims. More generally, threats to internal validity can be defined as the domain of factors that can lead to misestimating the counterfactual conditions used for local causal conclusions, a domain that is equally relevant for aggregate, moderated, and mediated causal claims.

The expanded domain of internal validity thus allows a sharper definition of external validity as concerned only with generalizing to units, settings, treatment, and outcomes not in the current study. This involves a well-defined set of threats to valid inference and is in line with Rossi, Lipsey, and Freeman (2004, p. 244) defining one aspect of causal generalization (i.e., the focus on treatments) as the "extent to which an impact assessment's findings can be extrapolated to similar programs or from the program as tested to the program as implemented."

Summary of Advantages of Dimensional Organization

Reframing types of valid inference in terms of intersecting dimensions offers several conceptual advantages. First, the dimensional approach encourages the more comprehensive coverage called for by House (this issue) by not relying on historically important discrete "types" of validity. It also avoids the possible overlap in the construct and external validity categories that concerns Reichardt (this issue). Further, defining the validity types in terms of intersecting dimensions supports considering an organization in terms of similarity of threats to validity, which in turn expands internal validity to covering an array of observation-based local causal conclusions.

The dimensional organization also clarifies the sequencing of how our understanding might best be pursued. In contrast to the sterile debates that Gargani and Donaldson (this issue) rightfully address regarding whether internal validity should always be the sine qua non and foundation for external validity, the multiple dimensions highlight the flexible options in developing our understanding. For example, there are times that moderated descriptive relationships in one context (such as gaps in academic achievement across demographic indicators) might profitably be studied in other contexts in pursuit of a generalized descriptive understanding, with internal validity regarding causal conclusions coming much later.

Thus, although we might ideally want understanding in every cell in Figure 5.2, this is not a responsible goal for any study, and there is no universal path of progression of understanding through the cells of Figure 5.2 to be pursued in streams of research—profitable approaches will depend on context. Further, even a single study can yield a progression of understanding when, for example, evidence indicating aggregate effectiveness of an outreach program for at-risk youth is further supported by making new predictions for mediated and moderated relationships (predictions which are not themselves entailed by the aggregate finding, and so not tautological) to be confirmed with the same data. This iteration between exploration and confirmation within the context of a single study, common in qualitative inquiry, is a form of context-confirmatory inquiry referred to as *principled discovery* (Julnes, 1995; Julnes & Mark, 1998).

Discussion

This chapter has considered a few ways that the Campbellian validity framework might be developed further to enhance its value to us. In reflecting on my recommendations and the broader discussion on this issue, it is useful to highlight the need for balance in how we approach validity frameworks.

Balance of Values-Neutral and Values-Engaged Perspectives

In that the language of valid inference can imply objectivity, Greene (2007; this issue) is right to remind us that researchers are inherently values engaged when conducting inquiry and that purportedly factual conclusions generally involve valuative elements (an earlier, longer version of this chapter addressed valuative validity as parallel, in Figure 5.2, to the descriptive and causal varieties). And so, acknowledging with Cronbach (1982, p. 108) that "validity is subjective rather than objective," we pursue valid inference not as a source of truth but rather for actionable evidence appropriate for decision making (Argyris, 1996; Julnes & Rog, 2008). Putnam (2002) provides a useful perspective on how evidence can be both "objective" enough to be actionable and also conditioned by values, arguing it is possible and appropriate to distinguish between primarily factual and value-based claims while still rejecting the fact–value dichotomy.

Balance Between Tradition and Innovation

Another needed balance concerns how we are to benefit from our rich conceptual inheritance regarding validity without becoming limited by it. Central to this concern is our awareness that the Campbellian approach was developed first for a specific focus and only later evolved into a general validity framework with implications for all research. We need to modify our validity frameworks as their applications evolve, but we also value continuity. In line with Neurath's metaphorical boat, which needs to be repaired while out at sea but only with the resources at hand, we cannot stop developing our validity frameworks, but we do not have the luxury of starting from scratch. Viewing validity in terms of intersecting dimensions, rather than as discrete types, is already part of the systemization of SCC; we need to continue its elaboration (Julnes, 2004).

Balance in Efforts Toward Systemization

A final balance to be addressed concerns the advantages and problems inherent in promoting more systematic approaches to validity. Maintaining a balance between admiration for and skepticism about this systematization was important in Pepper's (1942) distinction between dispersive and integrative theories. Whereas dispersive theories consist of lists (as in the somewhat unorganized early lists of threats to internal validity), integrative theories seek to identify fundamental distinctions in terms of underlying dynamics. Integrative, systematic frameworks, therefore, have the advantage of entailing better-developed implications that can lead to better insights and better practice. However, this integrative impulse can be poorly served if our understanding is inadequate—while we aim for conceptual distinctions that correspond to something more or less fundamental about the world, the hope of "carving nature at its joints"—such meaningful organization often eludes us (Julnes & Mark, 1998).

SCC capture this concern in saying that "although this new formulation in this book is definitely more systematic than its predecessors, we are unsure whether that systematization will ultimately result in greater terminological clarity or confusion" (p. 468). And so it is that the deliberate systematization of SCC is both a contribution and a source of controversy—their framework offers additional implications for guiding practice but also a clearer target for those with different visions. I argue that some form of systemization will continue, that it will involve viewing validity in terms of multiple, intersecting dimensions of valid inference, and that this will lead us to appreciate the multiple paths by which we elaborate our understanding and to reframe statistical conclusion validity as something like relational validity—if not now, then eventually. In the meantime, we need to encourage diversity in our conceptions and then promote meaningful discussion of advantages and disadvantages. SCC have made their choices, and the result is good. If this tradition is to remain vital and be of most use (including to qualitative researchers and other groups not currently embracing the framework), others need to step forward, as this chapter attempts to do, offering variations of the Campbellian vision based on other choices.

References

Argyris, C. (1996). Actionable knowledge: Design causality in the service of consequential theory. *Journal of Applied Behavioral Science, 32*(4), 390–406.

Campbell, D. T. (1986). Relabeling internal and external validity for applied social scientists. In W. M. K. Trochim (Ed.), *Advances in quasi-experimental design and analysis. New Directions for Program Evaluation, 31*, 67–77.

Campbell, D. T., & Stanley, J. C. (1963). *Experimental and quasi-experimental designs for research*. Chicago, IL: Rand McNally.

Cook, T. D., & Campbell, D. T. (1979). *Quasi-experimentation: Design and analysis issues for field settings*. Skokie, IL: Rand McNally.

Cronbach, L. J. (1982). *Designing evaluations of educational and social programs*. San Francisco: Jossey-Bass.

Greene, J. C. (2007). Method choices are contextual, contingent, and political. In G. Julnes & D. J. Rog (Eds.), *Informing federal policies on evaluation methodology: Building the evidence base for method choice in government sponsored evaluation. New Directions for Evaluation, 113*, 111–113.

House, E. (2008, November). *Reconsidering validity*. Paper presented at the annual American Evaluation Association conference in Denver, CO.

Julnes, G. (1995, July). *Tenth-generation evaluation: A context-confirmatory model for integration of practice and theory*. Paper presented at the Trinity Symposium, part of the Annual Meeting of the American Society for Public Administration, San Antonio, TX.

Julnes, G. (2004). Review of experimental and quasi-experimental designs for generalized causal inference by W. R. Shadish, T. D. Cook, & D. T. Campbell. *Evaluation and Program Planning, 27*(2), 173–185.

Julnes, G. (2008, November). *Reframing validity for fun and profit*. Paper presented at the annual American Evaluation Association conference in Denver, CO.

Julnes, G., & Mark, M. M. (1998). Evaluation as sensemaking: Knowledge construction in a realist world. In G. T. Henry, G. Julnes, & M. M. Mark (Eds.), *Realist evaluation: An emerging theory in support of practice. New Directions for Evaluation, 78*, 33–52.

Julnes, G., & Rog, D. J. (2007). Current federal policies and controversies over methodology in evaluation. In G. Julnes & D. J. Rog (Eds.), *Informing federal policies on evaluation methodology: Building the evidence base for method choice in government sponsored evaluation. New Directions for Evaluation, 113*, 1–12.

Julnes, G., & Rog, D. J. (2008). Evaluation methods for producing actionable evidence: Contextual influences on adequacy and appropriateness of method choice. In S. I. Donaldson, C. A. Christie, & M. M. Mark (Eds.), *What counts as credible evidence in applied research and evaluation practice?* (pp. 96–131). Thousand Oaks, CA: Sage.

King, G., Keohane, R. O., & Verba, S. (1994). *Designing social inquiry: Scientific inference in qualitative research.* Princeton, NJ: Princeton University Press.

Pepper, S. C. (1942). *World hypotheses: A study in evidence.* Berkeley, CA: University of California Press.

Putnam, H. (2002). *The collapse of the fact/value dichotomy.* Cambridge, MA: Harvard University Press.

Reichardt, C. (2008, November). *A critique of the Campbellian conception of validity and an alternative.* Paper presented at the annual American Evaluation Association conference in Denver, CO.

Remler, D. K., & Van Ryzin, G. G. (2011). *Research methods in practice: Strategies for description and causation.* Thousand Oaks, CA: Sage.

Rossi, P. H., Lipsey, M. W., & Freeman, H. E. (2004). *Evaluation: A systematic approach* (7th ed.). Thousand Oaks, CA: Sage.

Shadish, W. R., Cook, T. D., & Campbell, D. T. (2002). *Experimental and quasi-experimental designs for generalized causal inference.* Boston: Houghton Mifflin.

Shadish, W. R., Cook, T. D., & Leviton, L. C. (1991). *Foundations of program evaluation: Theories of practice.* Thousand Oaks, CA: Sage.

GEORGE JULNES is professor of public and international affairs in the College of Public Affairs at the University of Baltimore.

House, E. R. (2011). Conflict of interest and Campbellian validity. In H. T. Chen, S. I. Donaldson, & M. M. Mark (Eds.), *Advancing validity in outcome evaluation: Theory and practice. New Directions for Evaluation, 130,* 69–80.

6

Conflict of Interest and Campbellian Validity

Ernest R. House

Abstract

The conflicting interests of evaluators are biasing the findings of some evaluations and experiments, even technically rigorous studies. One improvement would be to emphasize evaluator and investigator conflict-of-interest threats in conceptions of validity. Such discussions could suggest ways to assess and avoid conflicts of interest. I explore the possibilities in one highly regarded framework, the Campbellian conception of experimental validity. However, all evaluations and experiments, whatever their methods, are vulnerable, and all conceptions of validity should address such threats. © Wiley Periodicals, Inc., and the American Evaluation Association.

When I reviewed the medical research literature a few years ago, I discovered statements in journals that the pharmaceutical drug evaluations under review were biased and that the same studies were high quality (House, 2008). What could this mean? How could the same studies be rigorous and biased simultaneously? What the reviewers seemed to mean was that the studies had randomized assignment and double-blind controls—markers of rigorous design—but were manipulated in other ways to produce positive results. Here are sources of bias in these studies.

Special thanks to G. Elsworth, G. Glass, D. Gorman, S. Lapan and his students, and M. Mark for help in shaping these ideas.

- Opportunistic choice of comparison (placebo rather than competitor)
- Improper choice of sample (younger subjects suffer fewer side effects)
- Manipulation of dosages (higher dosages for sponsor drugs)
- Incorrect administration of drugs (e.g., oral instead of injected)
- Manipulation of time scales (chronic-use drugs tested for short periods)
- Opportunistic outcome selection (ignoring possible side effects)
- Ignoring actual negative effects
- Redefining goals of study after findings to achieve success
- Opportunistic data analyses
- Opportunistic interpretations ("This drug is now the treatment of choice.")
- Concealing unfavorable data
- Control of authorship (company employees, rather than researchers, writing reports)
- Selective publishing (publishing only positive findings)
- Deceptive publishing (publishing positive findings repeatedly under different authors)

These biases are deliberate. That is, many drug evaluations are being designed and conducted to deliver positive findings (Angell, 2004). The studies are biased even while adhering to rigorous design safeguards. There is a sense in which rigorous methods, the way we normally think of them, are insufficient for claiming the studies are valid. That is not to say that rigorous methods are not necessary. In these late-stage clinical drug trials, there is no doubt that they are.

Drug evaluations are controlled by sponsoring companies for whom positive findings mean billions of dollars in profits. Testing a new drug for the market is risky and expensive. Drug companies bear the cost. And, apparently, leaving the results to honest evaluation is too chancy for some. Factors that strongly influence findings inappropriately include these:

Sponsorship of the study
Terms of the contract
Financial ties
Proprietary ties
Personal ties
Gifts

Indeed, vested interests have been shown empirically to influence findings (Als-Nielsen, Chen, Gluud, & Kjaergard, 2003). In spite of such evidence, some researchers claim that they are not influenced by the large sums of money paid by companies, nor are they influenced by holding patents. It does not help their credibility that many conceal their financial ties to companies.

How serious is the problem? In 2008 Senator Grassley held hearings comparing drug company payout records to fees medical researchers say they received. For example, from 2000 to 2007, Charles Nemeroff, an eminent psychiatrist and editor of *Psychopharmacology*, was chief investigator of a $3.9 million National Institutes of Health (NIH) grant that used Glaxo, Smith, Kline drugs. NIH rules require investigators to report income of $10,000 in any year to NIH and for universities to replace such investigators. Nemeroff reported earning $35,000 from Glaxo; actually he earned $960,000 (Harris, 2008). In total, he received $2.8 million from drug companies and failed to report $1.2 million of it. This is a violation of NIH rules. Child psychiatrist Joseph Biderman from Harvard Medical School and his colleague Timothy Wilkens reported receiving several hundred thousand dollars each from drug makers. Actually they earned $1.6 million each. Such researchers serve on panels that approve drugs. Senator Grassley said universities seem incapable of policing these conflicts of interest.

Drug evaluations are not the only manifestation of conflict of interest (COI). Gorman and colleagues conducted analyses showing conflicts of interest in the evaluation of school-based drug and violence prevention programs (Gorman, 2002, 2005; Gorman & Conde, 2007; Gorman, Conde, & Huber, 2007; Gorman & Huber, 2009). Evaluator independence was lacking in these studies, and the financial interests of the evaluators were affected by the findings. Studies contained questionable analyses, opportunistic changes in outcome variables, and weaknesses in selection and retention. Based on these studies the programs were placed on the Department of Education's list of evidence-based model programs. The push to be included on evidence-based recommendation lists has intensified conflicts of interest because the designation is marketable (Gorman, 2006).

In noting that drug-use prevention program findings had little validity, Moskowitz (1993) reported the studies suffered from conflicts of interest. Similarly, Eisner (2009) questioned disparities in findings from criminology studies done independently versus those done by evaluators with conflicts of interest. Although there are unresolved issues, it is safe to conclude that conflicts of interest are widespread and worsening (Feinstein, 1988; MacCoun, 1998).

Campbell and Stanley's Conception of Validity

One step to deal with conflict-of-interest threats would be to emphasize them in our conceptions of validity. My example here is the Campbell and Stanley conception of experimental validity and its later revisions, but these concerns apply to all conceptions of validity. As my colleagues in this issue note, Campbell and Stanley's typology is a conception of experimental validity, not of evaluation. However, Campbell and Stanley and approaches derived from it are used as the core of many evaluations, and these validity discussions influence evaluations employing experimental methods. Drug studies are both evaluations and experiments. Although I am focused on evaluations, similar considerations apply to experimental studies in which the stakes are high and variously sponsored, as with many environmental, biological, and ecological studies. Experimental studies are vulnerable to investigator conflict of interest, depending on circumstances.

The seminal work on experimental design is Campbell and Stanley (1963), followed by Cook and Campbell (1979) and Shadish, Cook, and Campbell (2002). I start with the original conception to illustrate that conceptions of validity are products of their time, that validity conceptions take shape from the situation, and that situations change. Here are the threats to validity enumerated in Campbell and Stanley (i.e., other effects confounded with treatment effects).

> History—events occurring between first and second measurements
> Maturation—processes occurring within respondents
> Testing—effects of test taking on later testing
> Instrumentation—changes in instruments, observers, and scorers
> Statistical regression—operates where groups are selected on extreme scores
> Biases—differential selection of respondents for comparison groups
> Experimental mortality—differential loss of respondents from groups
> Selection–maturation interactions
> Reactive or interactive effects of testing
> Interactive effects of selection biases and experimental variables
> Reactive effects of experimental treatment precluding generalization
> Multiple treatment interference

These threats are not deliberate. They are accidents and artifacts of experimental conditions. Colleagues inform me that Campbell was aware of potential investigator biases: ". . . scientists are thoroughly human beings: greedily ambitious, competitive, unscrupulous self-interested, clique-partisan, biased by tradition and cultural misunderstandings. . . ." (Campbell, 1984, p. 31). He goes on: "The complete sociology of applied-science validity . . . would take into account environmental impacts on commitments to validity which applied science careers involve" (Campbell, 1984, p. 41).

Why then wasn't conflict of interest included in the original framework? My view is that there was no reason to include it at the time. Conflicts of interest were not major threats. In the 1950s and 1960s it made good sense to ignore deliberate manipulation of findings. Perhaps we were too naïve, but the belief was that researchers aimed for findings that contributed to theory and practice. What was the point in manipulating findings? In any case, findings were subject to review and replication.

I did not emphasize conflict of interest in my work at the time, nor did most evaluators. The exception is Michael Scriven, who worried about government reporting (Scriven, 1976). In the 1980s the situation changed. Reagan began privatizing and deregulating many functions of government, including research and evaluation, trends that continued in ensuing administrations and led to a different environment.

Revised Conceptions

The original Campbellian conception of validity was brilliantly conceived, tremendously influential, and a product of its time. Campbell created the internal/external distinction because students mistakenly believed that Fisherian randomization controlled all threats to validity (Shadish et al., 2002, p. 37, footnote 3). Cook (2004) has explicated changes in conception in Cook and Campbell (1979) and Shadish et al. (2002).

In Shadish et al. (2002), the latest version, validity refers to the approximate truth of an inference. According to the authors, inferences from studies invariably involve human judgment and are not absolute or automatically derived. Nor are inferences guaranteed by particular methods or designs. The conception is pragmatic in that it emphasizes ruling out alternative explanations. Some threats can be recognized early and blunted by design controls. Others are not easily anticipated and must be considered *post hoc*. Researchers can investigate threats by asking how they apply in particular cases, whether they are plausible, and whether they operate in the same direction as program effects. Threats change over time, and their saliency varies from study to study. Lists of threats serve as useful heuristics for investigators, though such lists are not complete. I find this conception quite reasonable, without delving into the subcategories of statistical, internal, construct, and external validity. It is admirably flexible and allows for changing times.

The revised conception also fits my notion of how validity is determined generally. Determining validity requires evaluating the study itself. In analyzing the logic of evaluative argument, I suggested that evaluations consist of arguments that piece together strands of information, quantitative and qualitative, general and particular (House, 1977). Cronbach used this idea to recast standardized test validity, which at that time consisted of establishing correlations among test scores (Cronbach, 1989). He contended that test validation should be based on broad justifying arguments. The idea of validity based on arguments makes sense.

Elsworth (1994) extended the original conception in another direction. Working from Campbell's relabeling of internal validity as local molar causal validity, Elsworth applied a scientific realist view to validating field studies. For scientific realists social systems are open, and inferences are validated by explanatory power. In social systems unknown intervening causal interactions are always possible and often undetected. Elsworth also construed threats as plausible alternative explanations, with threats countered by design and post hoc analyses involving constructing arguments for and against (Dunn, 1982). Threats can be discovered by examining particular situations. Elsworth's conception is compatible with Shadish et al. (2002). (See Mark, Henry, & Julnes,

2000, for another conception based on scientific realism and Norris, 2005 for an overview of the concept of validity.)

Most discussions of validity do not emphasize conflict-of-interest threats. In Shadish et al. (2002), motivational threats to construct validity include these:

1. Self-report motivation
2. Participant perceptions of situation
3. Experimenter expectancies
4. Novelty and disruption effects
5. Compensatory equalization
6. Compensatory rivalry
7. Resentful demoralization

These threats result from participant motivations, not investigator motivations, except for experimenter expectations. The latter refers to Rosenthal's work on how experimenter expectations influence participants, not on how researchers deliberately bias findings. Elsworth included "coercion" of the investigator to perspectives of the group studied, addressing the danger of "going native," but not evaluator motivation to change findings because of self-interest. Remedies presented by Shadish et al. (2002) and by Elsworth include placebos, masking procedures, less obvious measures, delayed outcome measures, multiple experimenters, and minimizing contacts between researchers and participants.

Conflicts of interest are different kinds of threats that arise from the objective situation. They cause investigators to behave differently. Conflicts of interest require bringing the investigators themselves into the validity analysis. Some might argue that these threats should be handled outside validity frameworks, but that would leave these schema ignoring serious threats. To recite Campbell's concern about Fisherian randomization, the omission might lead students and others to think all threats are controlled when they are not. Others might argue that these threats can be handled solely through technical controls, but this remedy has not worked well in drug studies. A better solution is to address conflicts of interest directly. Judgments of validity should consider not only technical safeguards, but also the conflicts of interest of investigators.

Including Conflict-of-Interest Threats

How might such threats be included in the Shadish et al. (2002) conception of validity? The framework is an individual-psychological model of causal inference that posits investigators drawing inferences backed by evidence. Right now, it does not emphasize conflict of interest. As different kinds of threats, evaluator conflicts of interest can adversely affect anything in the evaluation, as the drug studies demonstrate, and be manifested in all four validity types. For example, drawing inappropriate conclusions might threaten external, internal, or construct validity. Tracking all such possibilities would require enormous effort.

Another way to address such threats would be to discuss whether the evaluator/investigator is without conflict at the beginning, to handle conflict of interest or its absence as an explicit assumption early on. Conflict-of-interest threats could be addressed at the front edge of the framework, so to speak, as an assumption that might be violated. That would keep the four validity types (statistical conclusion, internal, construct, and external) intact. By modifying the front part of the causal inference model, one could discuss conflicts of interest, how they can be discovered, and remedies for dealing with them. In other words, this is what happens when a key assumption is violated and how to remedy it.

Such an expansion of the conception makes sense theoretically, by placing the assumption where it fits the causal inference model, and practically, by treating conflict of interest threats succinctly without disturbing other components. (There might be other assumptions.) Cook (2004) noted that the Campbellian schema has sometimes valued practical fixes at the expense of building inconsistencies into major concepts. In this case there is no need for theoretical inconsistency. The proposed revision fits the causal inference model.

In my opinion, changes to the schema should be done by those who have deep tacit knowledge of the framework. Nonetheless (prodded by editors), I would enumerate conflict of interest threats and inquire if the evaluator/investigator harbors such conflicts. The relationship of the evaluator to sponsors and program is central. If conflicts of interests do obtain, I would ask if the study should proceed, or if underway or completed, whether the study should receive close independent scrutiny. I would explore remedies developed by those who have wrestled with these problems, such as the Food and Drug Administration (FDA), the medical journals, and the medical schools. Of course, these are suggestions. There may be better ways to handle such threats. The important point is to handle them somewhere in the framework.

Remedies

Strategies for dealing with conflicts of interest include transparency, oversight, and organization.

Transparency

Revealing conflicts of interest is critical. When participants serve on study panels for the National Academy of Sciences (NAS), they serve unpaid, a requirement set down by Abraham Lincoln when he founded the Academy (Feuer, 2009). Lincoln stipulated that the organization should serve the public and not merely enhance professional status. Panel members are asked to reveal potential conflicts of interest that might impair the task at hand. These written statements are reviewed by Academy staff and discussed by fellow panel members to determine how serious the conflicts might be.

For example, in a review of National Aeronautics and Space Administration (NASA) education programs, some panelists, particularly those with previous NASA affiliations, might have conflicts. One left the panel when he decided to bid on a NASA contract. Revealing such possibilities in writing is not an odious requirement, and similar safeguards would not be asking too much of evaluators. Transparency—revealing potential conflicts of interest— might be required for evaluators conducting studies, with written declarations part of the record.

Another transparency tactic would be to make data and methods accessible for criticism. Although transparency seems critical in any scientific endeavor, it is not always practiced. Indeed, drug companies often do not make data available, though they are formally required to do so.

Oversight

Revealing conflicts of interest voluntarily is not enough. For example, the credibility of NAS reviews is reinforced by oversight and organizational arrangements. First, the review is performed by a presumably impartial scientific organization. Second, panel members are chosen for expertise, and the panel is balanced with members representing different viewpoints. Third, the panel is given a formal charge, like a jury; most panelists take such charges seriously. Fourth, part of the charge is that panel members agree on a consensus report, if possible. This requirement forces members to engage in extended discussions and arguments. Serious deliberation leads to better-informed and more impartial findings (if done properly). Finally, the draft report is subject to external reviews.

The FDA requires advisory panel members to reveal conflicts of interest in writing, and these declarations are assessed by FDA staff (Committee on the Assessment of the US Drug Safety System, 2006). Panel members who receive $50,000 or more from a company with a product at issue are not allowed to serve. Those who receive less can serve, but are not allowed to vote on drug approval. Vioxx would not have been returned to the marketplace if this rule had been in effect (Harris, 2007). Ten of 32 advisers voting for approval would have been disqualified.

Some medical schools have restricted gifts to students and faculty (Moynihan, 2003). A recent study found medical students were influenced favorably toward products by simple gifts like coffee mugs and pens with the drug's name on them, even while believing they were not susceptible to influence (Nagourney, 2009). The American Medical Student Association endorses stricter guidelines such as limiting visits of drug representatives, restricting events sponsored by industry, and limiting journals accepting advertising (Moynihan, 2003).

Until recently, medical research journals regarded themselves as neutral conduits for scientific information, but several incidents have led to reassessment. The *New England Journal of Medicine* retracted a key article about Vioxx because Merck failed to include negative data about cardiovascular risk, though the missing data were reported to the FDA (Armstrong, 2006; Zimmerman & Tomsho, 2005). Eventually the drug was recalled. Missteps led the journal editors not to challenge the original manuscript. Drug advertising contributes significant journal revenue. The journal received $88 million in publishing revenue in 2005 and $697,000 from Merck for reprints of the Vioxx article.

Journal authors are asked to reveal financial ties and sign statements that they wrote the article. Company employees have been ghostwriting articles and having MDs sign (Singer, 2009). Journals also are requesting that all studies be registered in an NIH database so they can track studies never reported. Sometimes positive findings for drugs are published by different authors in different journals without cross-reference, as if these were separate studies. Without access to all studies, reviewers are likely to base recommendations on biased evidence unknowingly (Melander, Ahlqvist-Rastad, Meijer, & Beermann, 2003).

Organization

Often conflicts of interest arise from the organization of the evaluation enterprise. For example, drug companies have become involved in every aspect of studies (Bodenheimer, 2000). Companies hire contract research organizations to implement company designs, and these contract organizations are heavily dependent on the firms for funding (Bodenheimer, 2000). In the 1990s, the FDA began accepting user fees for clinical trials and negotiating with companies about how to do reviews, giving the industry leverage over the agency (Mathews, 2006).

The obstacles to honest evaluation are less obvious in the internal organization of the FDA (Committee on Assessment of the US Drug Safety System, 2006). Two offices inside are responsible for evaluating drugs. One oversees clinical trials; the other tracks long-term effects of drugs already on the market. Clinical trials receive most funding and authority because they make or break success initially. Also, the clinical-trial office employs higher-status research methods, whereas the follow-up office uses epidemiological methods to track effects.

The thousands of drugs on the market could all interact with each other. No clinical trial, no matter how huge, could anticipate interactions across all patients. Clinical trials necessarily focus on efficacy, not drug safety. An Institute of Medicine review recommended more funding and authority for the follow-up office, which is seriously underfunded (Committee on Assessment of the US Drug Safety System, 2006). These problems reside in the organization and interaction of the industry with its regulators.

Some time ago, Scriven (1976) posited three principles of organizational bias control. The principle of *independent feedback* is that no unit should rely entirely on a subunit for evaluative information about that subunit. The second principle, the *instability of independence*, is that independence is fleeting and subject to compromise. Hence, there must be arrangements for renewal and replacement as evaluators become co-opted. The third principle, *dynamic equilibrium*, is that although there are no totally unbiased evaluators, there are arrangements that can reduce the influence of the most damaging biases. "... independence is essential, impermanent, and situational" (Scriven, 1976, p. 139).

Scriven's clarification of the concept of "bias" is also worth reiterating. Sometimes bias refers to the systematic tendency to make errors and sometimes to actually making the errors. The former meaning is crucial in maintaining the credibility of evaluations while the latter affects validity. We need both credibility and validity. Conflicts of interest increase the tendency to commit errors. In spite of this evaluators sometimes conduct valid evaluations even when findings weigh against their own material interests. Unfortunately, the track record is not encouraging. By reducing conflict of interest—the potential for bias that gives rise to actual bias—we can improve both credibility and validity.

Summary

Although drug evaluations are technically rigorous, some are manipulated to produce favorable findings. Evaluator and investigator conflicts of interest are becoming increasingly serious and widespread. Our conceptions of validity do not emphasize conflict-of-interest threats, including the Campbell and Stanley conception of experimental validity and its later revisions. Including conflict-of-interest threats in validity frameworks is important—best to address such threats directly so everyone will be alerted. Such threats could be addressed in various places within the Campellian framework. One reason the tradition has endured nearly 50 years is that it has long-prized practical responses to new problems. Campbell noted, "A validity producing social system of science is nothing we should take for granted" (Campbell, 1984, p. 32). Of course, other validity conceptions should also address these threats.

References

Als-Nielsen, B., Chen, W., Gluud, C., & Kjaergard, L. L. (2003). Association of funding and conclusions in randomized drug trials. *Journal of the American Medical Association, 290*(7), 921.

Angell, M. (2004). *The truth about the drug companies.* New York: Random House.

Armstrong, D. (2006, May 15). How the New England Journal missed warning signs on Vioxx. *Wall Street Journal.*

Bodenheimer, T. (2000). Uneasy alliance: Clinical investigators and the pharmaceutical industry. *New England Journal of Medicine, 342*(20), 1539–1544.

Campbell, D. T. (1984). Can we be scientific in applied social science? In R. F. Connor, D. G. Altman, & C. Jackson (Eds.), *Evaluation studies review annual.* Beverly Hills, CA: Sage.

Campbell, D. T., & Stanley, J. C. (1963). *Experimental and quasi-experimental designs for research.* Chicago: Rand McNally.

Committee on the Assessment of the US Drug Safety System, A. Baciu, K. Stratton, & S. P. Burke (Eds.). (2006). *The future of drug safety: Promoting and protecting the health of the public.* Washington, DC: National Academies Press.

Cook, T. D. (2004). Causal generalization. In M. C. Alkin (Ed.), *Evaluation roots* (pp. 88–113). Thousand Oaks, CA: Sage.

Cook, T. D., & Campbell, D. T. (1979). *Quasi-experimentation: Designs and analysis issues for field settings.* Chicago: Rand McNally.

Cronbach, L. J. (1989). Construct validation after thirty years. In R. E. Linn (Ed.), *Intelligence: Measurement, theory, and politics* (pp. 147–171). Urbana, IL: University of Illinois Press.

Dunn, W. N. (1982). Reforms as arguments. *Knowledge: Creation, Diffusion, Utilization, 3,* 293–326.

Eisner, M. (2009). No effects in independent trials: Can we reject the cynical view? *Journal of Experimental Criminology, 5,* 163–183.

Elsworth, G. R. (1994). Arguing challenges to validity in field research. *Knowledge: Creation, Diffusion, Utilization, 15*(3), 321–343.

Feinstein, A. R. (1988). Fraud, distortion, delusion, and consensus: The problems of human and natural deception in epidemiologic science. *American Journal of Medicine, 84,* 475–478.

Feuer, M. (2009). *Science advice as procedural rationality: Reflections on the National Research Council.* London: London School of Economics, Centre for the Philosophy of Natural and Social Science.

Gorman, D. M. (2002). Defining and operationalizing "research-based" prevention: A critique (with case studies) of the US Department of Education safe, disciplined, and drug-free schools exemplary programs. *Evaluation and Program Planning, 25,* 295–302.

Gorman, D. M. (2005). Does measurement dependence explain the effects of the Life Skills Training program on smoking outcomes? *Preventive Medicine, 40,* 479–487.

Gorman, D. M. (2006). Conflicts of interest in the evaluation and dissemination of drug use prevention programs. In J. Kleinig & S. Einstein (Eds.), *Intervening in drug use: Ethical challenges* (pp. 171–187). Huntsville, TX: Sam Houston State University.

Gorman, D. M., & Conde, E. (2007). Conflict of interest in the evaluation and dissemination of "model" school-based drug and violence programs. *Evaluation and Program Planning, 30,* 422–429.

Gorman, D. M., Conde, E., & Huber, J. C., Jr. (2007). *Drug and Alcohol Review, 26,* 585–593.

Gorman, D. M., & Huber, J. C. (2009). The social construction of evidence-based drug prevention programs. *Evaluation Review, 33,* 396–414.

Harris, G. (2007, March 22). F.D.A. limits role of advisers tied to industry. *New York Times,* p. A1.

Harris, G. (2008, October 4). Top psychiatrist didn't report drug makers pay, files show. *New York Times,* p. A1.

House, E. R. (1977). *The logic of evaluative argument.* Los Angeles: University of California at Los Angeles, Center for the Study of Evaluation.

House, E. R. (2008). Blowback: Consequences of evaluation for evaluation. *American Journal of Evaluation, 29*(4), 416–426.

MacCoun, R. J. (1998). Biases in the interpretation and use of research results. *American Review of Psychology, 49,* 259–287.

Mark, M. M., Henry, G. T., & Julnes, G. (2000). *Evaluation.* San Francisco: Jossey-Bass.

Mathews, A. W. (2006, September 1). Drug firms use financial clout to push industry agenda at FDA. *Wall Street Journal,* p. A1.

Melander, H., Ahlqvist-Rastad, J., Meijer, G., & Beermann, B. (2003, May 31). Evidence b(i)ased medicine—Selective reporting from studies sponsored by pharmaceutical industry: Review of studies in new drug applications. *British Medical Journal, 326,* 1171–1173.

Moskowitz, J. M. (1993). Why reports of outcome evaluations are often biased or uninterpretable. *Evaluation and Program Planning, 16,* 1–9.

Moynihan, R. (2003). Who pays for the pizza? Redefining the relationships between doctors and drug companies. 2: Disentanglement. *British Medical Journal, 326,* 1193–1196.

Nagourney, E. (2009, May 19). Small gifts found to influence doctors. *New York Times,* p. D6.

Norris, N. (2005). Validity. In S. Mathison (Ed.), *Encyclopedia of evaluation* (pp. 439–442). Thousand Oaks, CA: Sage.

Scriven, M. (1976). Evaluation bias and its control. In G. V Glass (Ed.), *Evaluation studies review annual* (pp. 119–139). Beverly Hills, CA: Sage.

Shadish, W. R., Cook, T. D., & Campbell, D. T. (2002). *Experimental and quasi-experimental designs for generalized causal inference.* Boston: Houghton Mifflin.

Singer, N. (2009, August 5). Medical papers by ghostwriters pushed therapy. *New York Times,* pp. A1, B2.

Zimmerman, R., & Tomsho, R. (2005, May 26). Medical editor turns activist on drug trials. *Wall Street Journal,* p. B1.

ERNEST R. HOUSE is a professor emeritus of education at the University of Colorado.

Greene, J. C. (2011). The construct(ion) of validity as argument. In H. T. Chen, S. I. Donaldson, & M. M. Mark (Eds.), *Advancing validity in outcome evaluation: Theory and practice. New Directions for Evaluation, 130*, 81–91.

7

The Construct(ion) of Validity as Argument

Jennifer C. Greene

Abstract

The author presents an interpretive/constructivist perspective on outcome evaluation and on the warrants for our outcome-evaluation conclusions. The perspective underscores the importance of developing warrants through argumentation, in addition to selected empirical evidence. Congruencies with Don Campbell's visions of validity are noted. © Wiley Periodicals, Inc., and the American Evaluation Association.

House (this issue) reminds us that widely accepted conceptualizations of validity rest on the assumption of an objective, neutral evaluator. With this assumption, the challenges of maximizing the validity of our inferences are primarily methodological and procedural: Identify the major threats to validity, figure out how to control (for) these, and encourage evaluators to follow the steps thus prescribed. House's story, grounded in a critical review of pharmaceutical drug evaluations, challenges this assumption of neutrality with multiple accounts of inquirer and sponsor bias. House then offers an expansion of the Campbellian validity framework within which validity evidence and argument are marshaled to include investigator motivations at its "front edge."

The present chapter begins with the assumption that evaluators are neither neutral nor objective, but rather are inevitably and intrinsically *interested* inquirers. *Interested* for this discussion does *not* mean deliberately and intentionally biased, which is the major concern of House's argument. Rather, following the assumptions and stances of interpretive and constructivist approaches to social research and evaluation, *interested* implies a situated inquirer, one who inevitably brings to the process of social inquiry his or her own sociocultural history, beliefs about the social world and about what constitutes warranted knowledge of it, theoretical preferences, and moral and political values. There is no location outside one's own self—no "view from nowhere"—that permits an objective and disinterested view of social phenomena, their interrelationships, and their meanings. Thus, the knowledge and inferences claimed in an interpretivist study are inevitably imbued with the lenses and location of the particular inquirer. And thus, conceptualizations of the validity of inferences in interpretive traditions *must acknowledge* this inevitable influence of the particular inquirer on the data and the interpretations made thereof.

With a disinterested inquirer, validity represents an estimate of how closely one's inferences approximate an objective truth and is demonstrated primarily on methodological and procedural grounds. In interpretive traditions, the very concept of generalizable objective truth is contested—arising, in part, from assumptions about the importance of context, complexity, and contingency in understandings of the incidence, causes, and meaningfulness of human phenomena. And interpretive validity is not a matter of generating inferences that correspond to the real social world, but rather a matter of generating inferences that are meaningful, plausible, and of some consequence in the contexts at hand. The interpretive inquirer relies on procedural evidence related to validity, but more importantly turns to rhetorical persuasion and dialogic argument.

The discussion that follows engages two primary sets of issues. First, what are the interpretivist conceptualizations of validity as argumentation? Second, how do interpretive approaches to evaluation conceptualize and enact the two primary constructs in Campbell's typology, internal and external validity, or confidence in causal evaluative inferences and extrapolation of these inferences to other contexts (Cook & Campbell, 1979; Shadish, Cook, & Campbell, 2002)? The conclusion then underscores the continuities of these ideas from interpretive social science with the grand legacy of Donald Campbell's constructions of validity in evaluation.

But I first offer a brief interpretive perspective on outcome evaluation.

Making Interpretive Sense of Outcome Evaluation

This issue focuses on validity as relevant to outcome evaluations, specifically to the warrant for causal inferences and their generalizability. In the language of the editors, outcome evaluations "estimate the effect of a planned intervention such as a social or educational program (e.g., a supplementary instruction program) on one or more outcomes of interest (e.g., mathematics performance)." The focus on outcomes as isolatable phenomena that can be studied independently of processes and interactions is discordant with an interpretive view of the social world. Interpretivists, rather, perceive processes and outcomes as contextual and dynamic (changeable), as quite thoroughly entangled, and as constituting reciprocal influences on each other. So, studying an effect or outcome in isolation of its context and its mutually constitutive and multiple varying causes makes little interpretive sense. Changes in program participants' knowledge, attitudes, and/or behavior can only be interpreted sensibly with knowledge of the overall program experience.

Stake's (1995) case-study framework and his many responsive case-study evaluations well illustrate the interpretivist's sense making of outcomes. One such evaluation assessed the *quality* of a new training module for rating specialists in the Veterans Benefits Administration (VBA) (Stake, 1999, 2000). Rating specialists are highly trained professionals who review the benefits claims (and appeals) of veterans and determine the compensation owed to the claimant. The new module was designed to help raters do their work more efficiently and effectively in order to deal with a huge backlog of claims appeals. Phase I of this evaluation assessed the contextual quality of the module's design and implementation, using document review, interviews, site visits, and a national survey of trainees and their supervisors. Phase II centered on the longer-term performance of the module trainees and included assessments of noticeable changes in the appeals process from the perspective of raters, their supervisors, and veterans themselves. Methods for Phase II included site visits, phone interviews with veterans, surveys of staff in regional veterans' organizations, and analyses of existing data.

Quality in this evaluation was conceptualized as a holistic, multifaceted, contextual, dynamic phenomenon related to the intertwined aspects of the module's design, implementation, experience by trainees, and practical consequences for veterans' organization staff and veterans themselves. Meaningful and credible interpretation of Phase II data required an understanding of how the module was experienced by trainees and supported by their supervisors in specific workplaces, of rating specialists' job stresses and strains, of the role of the VBA in veterans' lives and the challenges invoked by a denied benefits claim, of the work climate of the various offices of the VBA, and more. Warranted interpretive understanding is contextual, holistic, and integrative.

Validity as Argument

This section deliberates the construction of validity as argument. Specific connections to validity in outcome evaluations are addressed in the next section.

The idea of validity as primarily a matter of argument, constructed rhetorically from evidence and shared conversations, is familiar to social scientists in many corners of the community, from postmodern scholars

(Lather, 1993) to psychometricians (Kane, 2006). The idea of validity as argument is also consonant with Campbell's own validity legacy. Campbell fully recognized that just as data analyses do not conveniently spit out conclusions and inferences in final form (rather, the evaluator must infer and "construct" these from the analysis results), neither does the evidence from validity procedures such as predictor–outcome correlations automatically constitute validity. The need to align, integrate, and interpret evidence into a convincing argument regarding validity has long been recognized in multiple evaluation traditions as an evaluator responsibility. What is distinctive about interpretive approaches to evaluation are (a) the other dimensions of persuasive inferences that are invoked as part of the argumentation and (b) the balance of evidence and argument presented.

As noted, validity as argument is invoked in interpretive traditions because interpretivists aspire not to objective truth per se, but rather to provisional, contingent, dynamic understandings about human action in context. Given this epistemological indeterminacy (Lather, 2001), interpretive evaluators draw on three other dimensions of the evaluation process to construct arguments about the validity of or warrant for inferences from an evaluation study, in addition to empirical evidence: (a) the contextual dimensions of human action, (b) the relational and dialogic facets of evaluation, and (c) the values that are central to the evaluation enterprise.

Drawing on Context

In interpretive traditions, context is understood as constitutive of meaning. That is, context is not simply the place in which the human activities of focus in an evaluation occur. Nor is it best conceptualized as a moderator or mediator of human action, that is, something separate from the action itself. Rather, the characteristics and qualities of a particular context—social, cultural, economic, material, organizational, and so forth—contribute to shaping actions and interactions in particular ways. So, context is an interwoven part of the data gathered and the inferences constructed. And so, appeals to the particular contextualities of interpretive evaluation inferences become part of the validity argument.

For example, envision an interpretivist evaluation of a school-based obesity-prevention program for middle school children that includes both nutrition education and considerable increases in the physical-activity portions of the school day. The program was implemented for all grade levels in all middle schools of an urban school district. Observations and interviews might yield the following kind of contextualized inference about children's engagement with the program:

> Many children appeared to be highly engaged with the program. These children demonstrated keen interest in the information provided about the nutritional content of foods that were highly familiar to them—part of their daily

diets and family traditions. And they delighted in spending part of their school day playing versions of hopscotch, jump rope, and street soccer that were also familiar to them, even using the rules for taking turns and selecting teams that the children themselves used. The program form and content, that is, validated important parts of children's lives that heretofore were absent from the school day. This validation appeared to be central to the children's engagement and active program participation.

Drawing on Relationships

Evaluation is fundamentally a social and relational craft (Abma, 2006; Schwandt, 2002). Evaluation takes place in real-world contexts that are threaded throughout with diverse interests, investments, and stakes. And it takes place via interactions with people who represent these diverse interests. For the interpretivist evaluator, these interactions and their broader relationships are vital to the conduct and the integrity of the work. The interpretivist evaluator is an up-close, on-site, engaged inquirer, privileging direct observation and conversation over standardized measurement, and actively nurturing relationships with multiple stakeholders as integral to the responsiveness, usefulness, *and* the quality of the evaluation that is conducted and the inferences generated. Frequent communications of multiple kinds with stakeholders, formal and informal progress reports, a regular evaluative presence on site, ongoing conversations about the meanings of interesting data that have surfaced—these are the core of the relational dimensions of interpretive evaluation.

And further, "our judgments of goodness are [in part] practical accomplishments, undertaken within the context of [ongoing] dialogue and persuasion, that we work out as we go along" (Smith, 1992, p. 103). Evaluative inferences that respect the conversations held along the way, as well as the dialogic norms of listening well and striving to understand the other (Greene, 2005), are inferences with stronger credibility and leverage among key stakeholders in the context at hand.

Drawing on Values

Evaluation is intrinsically judgmental and thus values engaged. The primary purpose of evaluation is to render judgments of merit and worth that are grounded in defensible empirical evidence and argument and that are anchored in chosen values. These values are most clearly articulated in the criteria used to make such judgments. The quality of an educational program, for example, can be judged on the extent of student agency in the curriculum, on student test-based achievement, or on teacher use of culturally appropriate pedagogy. Each criterion reflects different values, as well as different stakeholder interests.

Evaluators in interpretive traditions accept values as present in the phenomena we study, in the evaluative judgments we make, and also in the very data we generate—the latter due to the inevitably *interested* nature of our lenses. Many interpretive evaluators take a multipartisan or pluralistic position (for example, Stake, 2004), seeking to surface the value stances and claims of multiple stakeholders in the contexts being studied and enable stakeholder conversations about them. And more explicitly ideologically oriented evaluators—notably, those in the democratic (House and Howe, 1999), participatory (Whitmore, 1998), and culturally responsive (Hood, 2001; Thomas and Stevens, 2004) traditions—are openly partisan through the adoption of prescriptive value stances. *Yet*, these value stances pertain not to the program being evaluated per se, but rather to the political and action-oriented consequences of the program. That is, the advancement of these values is in service to the intended beneficiaries of the program being evaluated. To illustrate, a good program for democratic evaluators is one that advances the interests of those least well served in the contexts at hand and thus the democratic values of justice and equity.

As part of the process of warranting inferences, the interpretive evaluator's arguments also appeal to values. An inference can gain strength through an argument that references the value dimensions of the program and policy being evaluated, that invokes the value strands of evaluative conversation held along the way, and that demonstrates respect for and acceptance of multiple value claims and stances. The interpretive evaluator's own values can be— carefully and judiciously (that is, prescriptively)—part of the argument. Yet, because evaluation is a social practice concerned with real and consequential phenomena, the evaluator's primary responsibilities are to stakeholders in all their pluralities and multiplicities. In this sense, our validity arguments can help "protect our work from our passions" (Lather, 1986, p. 77).

Summary

Validity in interpretive evaluation is as much a process as an accomplishment, and involves as much argumentation and reasoning as it does empirical procedures and evidence. Although validity in all evaluation traditions requires both argument and evidence, interpretive evaluators likely rely relatively more on persuasive communications than empirical data. And this persuasion is enacted through appeals to critical strands of interpretive work—the contextuality of meaning and meaningfulness, the relational webs of evaluation in action, and the values that distinguish and ground our work.

The next section takes up the interpretive standpoints on more familiar ways of thinking about and accomplishing validity as relevant to outcome evaluations.

Familiar and Unfamiliar Validities

Of shared importance to all outcome evaluations are the internal and external validity components of Donald Campbell's typology. The distinguished

authors of most of the other chapters in this issue are engaging with perceived limitations to this typology and needs for reframing, updating, or
augmenting some of Campbell's original ideas about warrants for our evaluative conclusions about program outcomes.

Interpretivist evaluators also want to have confidence that our conclusions and inferences accurately and meaningfully convey what has happened
in the evaluation context and with what importance and implications. But
this confidence is not anchored in the narrow Campbellian sense of valid
causal inferences or in the broader realist correspondence notion of truth.
For interpretivists, veracity is not a matter of ruling out all plausible threats
to internal validity or establishing the correspondence of conclusions to the
real social world. Rather, internal validity warrants for interpretivist inferences to engage the plausibility, depth, relevance, and meaningfulness of the
interpretations rendered and the understandings reached (Wolcott, 1990).

Interpretivist evaluators also are concerned about the extent to which
our inferences themselves travel—to contexts and people other than those
studied—but the concern takes different form from the Campbellian construct of external validity.

The discussion that follows briefly reviews the primary interpretive versions of internal and external validity used in evaluation practice. As will be
evident, these again rely less on following accepted procedures or gathering
particular evidence, and more on persuasion and argument. The specific procedures discussed represent advice for the interpretivist evaluation practitioner.

"Yes, That Makes Sense to Me" or "My Own Experiences Were Similar"

The trustworthiness criteria for interpretive-constructivist (then "naturalistic") evaluation proposed by Guba and Lincoln (1989; Lincoln and Guba,
1985) have been soundly criticized by inquirers from all sides (for example,
Smith, 1992, and Phillips, 1987), but still endure as criteria of currency and
value for interpretive evaluators. This is largely because these criteria remain
close to conventional inquiry criteria and are thus relatively familiar to and
understandable by key evaluation stakeholders. They are also practical
and workable criteria. In the trustworthiness framework, internal validity
is reframed as credibility, which refers to the extent to which and ways in
which evaluation conclusions and inferences make sense to the people
in the context studied. Credible inferences capture important strands of
experiential meaningfulness of the evaluand in context. They offer a rendering of the program logic, implementation, and outcomes that resonates
with insiders' own experiences and understandings.

Guba and Lincoln further offered various procedures that could be used
to assess and strengthen the credibility of evaluative inferences. These include
prolonged engagement in the site—to aid in observational and interpretive
acuity—and peer debriefing, negative case analysis, and member checks—all
of which focus on sharpening inferences and checking or validating them

against data and with various constituencies. Negative case analysis, for example, involves the iterative checking of preliminary conclusions against various sets of data and revising such conclusions when contradictory or disconfirming evidence is presented. With this procedure, credible inferences have no major negative cases or contradictions in the data. As a second example, member checks involve checking preliminary conclusions against the experiences and understandings of key stakeholder groups, so that credible inferences are endorsed as plausible and meaningful by critical stakeholders.

Clearly, these procedures are anchored in interpretive processes and judgments, invoking evidence, but evidence in dialogue with argument and reason. That is, evidence about credibility does not directly lead to a claim of credibility, but rather must be engaged in dialogue through which a persuasive case about credibility may be made.

"These Findings Are Also Relevant to My Context, Which is Similar to That Studied" or "These Findings Have Important Substantive Implications for My Own Work in This Area"

As discussed earlier, central to an interpretive view of the world are the constitutive contributions of context to evaluation inferences. Further, because context is viewed as unique, dynamic, and contingent, evaluation inferences are also bounded by or even limited to the contexts under study. The postpositivist aspiration of statistical generalization from samples to a population, controlling for or holding contextual influences constant (external validity), is thus not sensible in an interpretive stance. Yet evaluators usually have obligations to generate inferences that extend beyond the particular contexts, times, and individuals studied.

Interpretivist evaluators have several responses to this challenge, all of which involve a conceptual or rhetorical argument about the applicability of particular evaluation inferences to contexts, activities, or ideas elsewhere and at other times. First, as part of the trustworthiness framework, Guba and Lincoln proposed the concept of transferability as an interpretive counterpart to external validity. Transferability refers to the applicability of the evaluative conclusions to other contexts, and it is a judgment of the evaluation user, not the evaluator. The evaluator's responsibilities then are to provide sufficient detailed contextual and programmatic description to enable the user to assess the likelihood of transfer. Second, Stake and Trumbull (1982) offered the idea of naturalistic generalization, again achieved by the reader or user, in this case via sufficient vicarious experiencing of the program in context. The evaluator's responsibility here is to provide rich, contextualized, emotive descriptions of the program as experienced by various stakeholders. Third, Firestone (1993), among others, offered the notion of analytic generalization for interpretive inquirers, which involves linking the findings of the particular case to a broader set of constructs or a theory, say a program theory in an evaluation context. "What have we learned about problem-based learning in mathematics for middle school children from this evaluation?" is an example of an analytic generalization question.

Enter the Notion of "Inference Quality"

A validity construct less familiar to evaluators is that of "inference quality" (Teddlie & Tashakkori, 2003), an idea that comes from the field of mixing methods and that is situated at the intersection of traditionally quantitative and traditionally qualitative methodologies. Inference quality presumes methodological quality, which in mixed methods studies is judged by the criteria relevant to the different methodologies included in the study. A pre-ordinate survey is methodologically judged by its response rates, standard errors, internal consistencies, and item clarity. An open-ended observation is methodologically judged by its comprehensiveness, capturing of diverse insider perspectives, descriptive detail, and perhaps evocative vignettes. But how do we judge the warrants for an evaluative inference that comes from an integration of these survey and observation data?

Several decades ago, Louis (1982) wondered the same thing in a large-scale educational evaluation of school leadership. To address the challenges of high rates of missing data, her team used existing data and considerable deliberation over two intensive days to construct a consolidated numerical data set for each of the participating schools. Louis then asked:

> Can a database composed of numbers that is entirely dependent on the iterative, holistic judgments of experienced site field teams be described as only quantitative? While the analysis procedures used to manipulate the data are statistical, the data itself [sic], and any interpretation of results is totally conditioned by its origins. On the other hand, as we approach any given analysis using case materials rather than quantified data, it has become genuinely impossible not to embed that activity in our knowledge of the descriptive statistics and correlational relationships that were available to us well before data collection had ended. (p. 21)

The validity of the conclusions and inferences in Louis's study well represent contemporary validity challenges in integrated mixed methods evaluation. Enter the nascent construct of inference quality. For Teddlie and Tashakkori (2003), inference quality includes conceptual consistency, interpretive agreement, and interpretive distinctiveness, which collectively privilege evidence and agreement, as well as the traditional concern of ruling out other plausible explanations for the results obtained. A broader and more balanced construal of the inference-quality construct could embrace argument alongside evidence, divergence alongside agreement, contextual understanding alongside causal explanations, and—especially important for evaluation—inclusion of the uses and action consequences of the inferences rendered.

Reprise

Worrying about warrant is a core evaluator responsibility. It is because our inferences are consequential that we must have confidence that they are warranted. This chapter has advanced the idea that strong warrants go beyond procedures and procedural evidence to an engagement with argument, dialogue, and conversation. This idea of reasoning in concert with evidence and especially in concert with others about the substance of and warrant for a given evaluation conclusion is fully continuous with Campbell's seminal ideas about validity. As much as any other aspect of social inquiry, Campbell valued ongoing and open critique of inquiry results and their warrants and advocated for the importance of warrants generated through the "disputatious community of scholars."

References

Abma, T. A. (2006). The social relations of evaluation. In I. F. Shaw, J. C. Greene, & M. M. Mark (Eds.), *The Sage handbook of evaluation* (pp.184–199). London: Sage.

Cook, T. D., & Campbell, D. T. (1979). *Quasi-experimentation: Design and analysis issues for field settings*. Chicago: Rand McNally.

Firestone, W. A. (1993). Alternative arguments for generalizing from data as applied to qualitative research. *Educational Researcher, 22*(4), 16–23.

Greene, J. C. (2005). Evaluators as stewards of the public good. In S. Hood, R. K. Hopson, & H. T. Frierson (Eds.), *The role of culture and cultural context: A mandate for inclusion, truth, and understanding in evaluation theory and practice. Evaluation and Society Series* (pp. 7–20). Greenwich, CT: Information Age Publishing.

Guba, E. G., & Lincoln, Y. S. (1989). *Fourth generation evaluation*. Newbury Park, CA: Sage.

Hood, S. L. (2001). Nobody knows my name: In praise of African American evaluators who were responsive. In J. C. Greene & T. A. Abma (Eds.), *Responsive evaluation. New Directions for Evaluation, 92,* 31–43.

House, E. R., & Howe, K. R. (1999). *Values in evaluation and social research*. Thousand Oaks, CA: Sage.

Kane, M. (2006). Validation. In R. L. Brennan (Ed.), *Educational measurement* (4th ed., pp. 17–64). New York: American Council on Education, and Macmillan.

Lather, P. (1986). Issues of validity in openly ideological research. *Interchange, 17*(4), 63–84.

Lather, P. (1993). Fertile obsession: Validity after poststructuralism. *The Sociological Quarterly, 34*(4), 673–693.

Lather, P. (2001). Validity as an incitement to discourse: Qualitative research and the crisis of legitimation. In V. Richardson (Ed.), *Handbook of research on teaching* (4th ed., pp. 241–250). Washington, DC: American Educational Research Association.

Lincoln, Y. S., & Guba, E. G. (1985). *Naturalistic inquiry*. Beverly Hills, CA: Sage.

Louis, K. S. (1982). Sociologist as sleuth: Integrating methods in the RDU study. *American Behavioral Scientist, 26*(1), 101–120.

Phillips, D. C. (1987). Validity in qualitative research: Why the worry about warrant will not wane. *Education and Urban Society, 20,* 9–24.

Schwandt, T. A. (2002). *Evaluation practice reconsidered*. New York: Peter Lang.

Shadish, W. R., Cook, T. D., & Campbell, D. T. (2002). *Experimental and quasi-experimental designs for generalized causal inference*. Boston: Houghton Mifflin.

Smith, J. K. (1992). Interpretive inquiry: A practical and moral activity. *Theory Into Practice, 31*(2), 100–106.

Stake, R. E. (1995). *The art of case study research.* Thousand Oaks, CA: Sage.

Stake, R. E. (1999, 2000). *Evaluation of the VBA Appeals Training Module, Certify a Case to the Board of Veteran Appeals. Evaluation Report* (Phase I, Phase II). Urbana-Champaign: University of Illinois, CIRCE.

Stake, R. E. (2004). *Standards-based and responsive evaluation.* Thousand Oaks, CA: Sage.

Stake, R. E., & Trumbull, D. J. (1982). Naturalistic generalizations. *Review Journal of Philosophy and Social Science, 7*(1), 1–12.

Teddlie, C., & Tashakkori, A. (2003). Major issues and controversies in the use of mixed methods in the social and behavioral sciences. In A. Tashakkori & C. Teddlie (Eds.), *Handbook of mixed methods in social and behavioral research* (pp. 3–50). Thousand Oaks, CA: Sage.

Thomas, V. G., & Stevens, F. I. (Eds.). (2004). *Co-constructing a contextually responsive evaluation framework. New Directions for Evaluation, 101.*

Whitmore, E. (Ed.). (1998). *Understanding and practicing participatory evaluation. New Directions for Evaluation, 80.*

Wolcott, H. (1990). On seeking—and rejecting—validity in qualitative research. In E. Eisner & A. Peshkin (Eds.), *Qualitative inquiry in education: The continuing debate* (pp. 121–152). New York: Teachers College Press.

JENNIFER C. GREENE is a professor of educational psychology at the University of Illinois at Urbana-Champaign.

8

Assessing Program Outcomes From the Bottom-Up Approach: An Innovative Perspective to Outcome Evaluation

Huey T. Chen, Paul Garbe

Abstract

The traditional top-down approach to program outcome evaluation stresses the need for strong evidence to establish an intervention's effectuality. This approach's principles and methodology are rooted in Campbellian typology and have been applied intensively in outcome evaluation. Yet lessons learned from such applications suggest that in addressing stakeholders' interests and needs, this approach has limitations. To be stakeholder responsive, evaluation must go beyond the top-down approach's focus and strategies. This chapter proposes an integrative validity model and a bottom-up approach as an alternative perspective to outcome evaluation. The new perspective enables evaluations to meet both scientific and practical requirements and enhances evaluations' usefulness. © Wiley Periodicals, Inc., and the American Evaluation Association.*

When conducting outcome evaluations for intervention programs (Rossi, Lipsey, & Freeman, 2004), evaluators traditionally have applied concepts, principles, and methods proposed in the

---

Disclaimer: The findings and conclusions of this article are those of the authors and do not necessarily represent the official position of the Centers for Disease Control and Prevention (CDC).

NEW DIRECTIONS FOR EVALUATION, no. 130, Summer 2011 © Wiley Periodicals, Inc., and the American Evaluation Association. *This article is a US Government work and, as such, is in the public domain in the United States of America. Published online in Wiley Online Library (wileyonlinelibrary.com) • DOI: 10.1002/ev.368

Campbellian validity typology (Campbell & Stanley, 1963; Cook & Campbell, 1979; Shadish, Cook, & Campbell, 2002). But as discussed in this issue's introduction (Chen, Donaldson, & Mark, this issue), Campbell and his colleagues developed the Campbellian validity typology for experimental research rather than for program evaluation. That the typology was intended for research does not mean evaluators cannot apply it to evaluation. But it does mean that when employing Campbellian typology, evaluators have to pay careful attention to such issues as

How has this application been conducted?
How well does this application serve outcome evaluation?
Can we use this experience to build a better evaluation alternative?

The evaluation literature has not systematically discussed these issues. This chapter intends to:

Examine the application of the Campbellian typology to the evaluation of health promotion/social betterment programs.
Use lessons learned to develop a more comprehensive validity perspective for program evaluation.
Incorporate a bottom-up approach into program evaluation.
Explain how integrative validity can improve outcome evaluation.

The Top-Down Approach to Validity Issues

The top-down approach represents a systematical application of the principles and methodology provided by the Campbellian validity typology in evaluating health promotion/social betterment programs (Chen, 2010).

The top-down approach is to evaluate an intervention in a sequential order from efficacy evaluation to effectiveness evaluation. According to this approach, an innovative intervention must undergo an efficacy evaluation to maximize internal validity in the assessment (Flay et al., 2005). The efficacy evaluation assesses intervention effects in an ideal and controlled setting. To maximize internal validity—that is, to provide the strongest evidence on whether an intervention is efficacious—the evaluation typically uses randomized controlled trials (RCTs). After the intervention's efficacy is determined, a real-world effectiveness evaluation is applied to address the evaluation's external validity (generalizability) issues. Only after an intervention proves efficacious in a controlled setting and effective in the real world is that intervention ready for dissemination.

Biomedical research has long used the top-down approach successfully. Many scientists regard this approach as the true path to scientific validity (Food and Drug Administration, 1992). And because of the top-down approach's scientific reputation, many funding agencies, researchers, and health promotion and social betterment program evaluators are attracted to it.

NEW DIRECTIONS FOR EVALUATION • DOI: 10.1002/ev

Lessons Learned From Applying the Top-Down Approach in Program Evaluation

The top-down approach's major contributions to program evaluation include establishment of stringent standards and concrete methods for enhancing precision in outcome evaluation. This approach has improved program evaluation's scientific reputation by proposing a use of RCTs to provide the strongest source of credible evidence of an intervention's effects. In fact, the term *evidence-based interventions* is often limited only to RCT-evaluated interventions. Yet in applying the top-down approach, health promotion/social-betterment programs have experienced the following problems.

The Conditions for Designing and Administering an Evidence-Based Intervention Often Do Not Resemble or Are Irrelevant to Real-World Operations

When assessing an intervention's effect, one efficacy evaluation purpose is to create an ideal and controlled setting to maximize internal validity. The problem, however, is that creation of an ideal and controlled setting in health promotion/social betterment programs decreases the intervention's real-world relevancy. Types of implementers illustrate the issue. To assure an intervention's appropriate delivery, highly qualified and enthusiastic implementers often provide the efficacy evaluation. But, as demonstrated in Open Airways for Schools (OAS), these implementers tend to have little resemblance to their real-world counterparts. OAS is a school-based health education program devised to enhance third–six graders' ability to manage their asthma on a daily basis. Designers intended that the program would facilitate the ability of parents and children to work with their clinicians to manage the disease. An efficacy evaluation in fact found that in attaining program goals, the intervention was efficacious (D. Evans, Clark, & Feldman, 1987). But then, the team delivering the OAS intervention comprised, among others, doctoral-level sociologists and educators with master's degrees in public health and social sciences (Bruzzese, Markman, Appel, & Webber, 2001). These highly qualified OAS counselors in the efficacy evaluation only remotely resembled real-world OAS counselors. In the real world, volunteer educators deliver OAS programs. These are parents with limited OAS training or limited training in behavioral change generally. Many community-based organizations cannot afford to hire highly qualified counselors. Thus stakeholders may view efficacy evaluation evidence as irrelevant to real-world situations.

Originally, use of highly qualified counselors in efficacy evaluations may have been intended to enhance internal validity. But the manipulation of research conditions and setting also creates an environment that boosts intervention effects. Highly qualified counselors usually have better knowledge and skills than real-world counselors in changing clients' beliefs or behaviors. From the real-world standpoint then, highly qualified and enthusiastic counselors in an efficacy evaluation may artificially inflate the intervention's desirable effects.

Note, however, that different types of counselors are only one of many contextual factors that could be manipulated in efficacy evaluation. Other contextual factors include monetary or other incentives provided to participants. Moreover, such factors as supervision, coordination, and recruitment process could also be manipulated to boost intervention effects. Unfortunately, when estimating an intervention effect, the literature on evidence-based interventions usually emphasizes methodological rigor and statistical precision. It largely ignores the issue that a creation of an ideal research setting such as recruiting motivated participants, employing highly trained and enthusiastic counselors, or using a talent management team might contribute to desirable effects (Chen, 1990, 2005). This might give audiences who are unaware of any unrealistic arrangements and possibly inflated effects a false impression or hope that application of these evidence-based interventions alone would result in similarly desirable real-world outcomes.

Evidence-Based Interventions Do Not Address Practical or Service Issues Highly Relevant to Stakeholders

Stakeholders are responsible for contacting and delivering services to clients in a day-to-day basis. Stakeholders have concerns about practical issues, such as whether an intervention would be attractive to real-world clients, whether the intervention would be suitable for ordinary implementers to deliver, and whether a typical community organization would be capable of managing the intervention. Although from a researcher's standpoint these practical issues may be regarded as trivial, to stakeholders they are crucial. Yet in efficacy evaluations these issues often are not addressed. This is another example of why, because most evidence-based interventions do not adequately address practical issues, stakeholders generally do not find them useful (Wandersman et al., 2008).

The need for evaluation to address stakeholders' views and concerns is clearly reflected in the four standards of program evaluation: utility, feasibility, propriety, and accuracy (Joint Committee on Standards for Educational Evaluation, 1994). Current forms of evidence-based interventions mainly focus on the fourth standard and do not adequately address the first three standards, which are concerned primarily with practical and service issues. This difference in focus results in a huge gap between intervention research and real-world practice (Chen, 2005; Green & Glasgow, 2006). Today more and more practitioners, decision makers, and consumers find that traditional scientific evaluation results tend not to be useful to the everyday issues about which those groups are concerned (Wandersman et al., 2008).

Evidence-Based Interventions Are Difficult to Implement in the Real World

As discussed previously, stakeholders' low enthusiasm for evidence-based interventions does not imply they do not put evidence-based interventions into practice. Because of funding-agency requirements, community-based organizations often implement evidence-based interventions. Just as often, however, when community-based organizations attempt to implement evidence-based interventions, they encounter real-world challenges. The difficulties are illustrated in the real-world implementation of the National Cooperative Inner-City Asthma Study (NCICAS). NCICAS was a randomized clinical trial of an intervention that used trained master's-level social workers to provide services to families for asthma counseling and to deal with the families' psychosocial needs (R. Evans et al., 1999). The RCT had the following features, typical in efficacy evaluation. Participants were provided with

Monetary and child-care incentives
Highly committed counselors
Food/refreshments
Counseling sessions at regular office hours
Frequent contacts for services

The evaluation did find the NCICAS intervention efficacious in reducing asthma morbidity among inner-city children.

The Inner-City Asthma Intervention (ICAI) wanted to implement the NCICAS intervention in a real-world setting (Kattan, 2006; Williams & Redd, 2006). But ICAI experiences demonstrated the difficulty of delivering the exact NCICAS intervention in the real world; in fact, many adaptations or changes were required. For example, ICAI social workers were unable to contact and meet with families as frequently as in NCICAS. The great majority of ICAI counseling sessions were held in the evenings, weekends, or both, in an attempt to promote continued participation in the intervention. Because of budget constraints, ICAI could not provide monetary and child-care incentives to clients and food/refreshments to increase the enjoyment of session attendance, as did NCICAS. ICAI also found retaining social workers difficult. Because of these implementation difficulties, at the end only 25% of the children in ICAI completed the entire intervention.

As shown in the ICAI experience, a common mechanism stakeholders use to cope with implementation difficulties is to modify an evidence-based intervention to fit a specific situation or need. The modification often means an adaptation or even a reinvention of an evidence-based intervention. For example, recipients of HIV prevention funding were required to implement evidence-based interventions such as VOICES/VOCES and MPower (Veniegas, Kao, & Rosales, 2009). In spite of stressing fidelity in the announcement, the community-based organizations in the study considerably modified key characteristics or redesigned evidence-based interventions. Changes included modification of the number and duration of sessions, addition of extra elements, and modification of the intervention content and delivery methods. The adaptations and reinventions were carried out during preimplementation, implementation, and maintenance phases.

Because of adaptation or reinvention, an evidence-based intervention and its real-world counterpart tend to differ substantially. And two versions of an intervention can create confusion in understanding, communicating, or disseminating intervention. Such questions arise as: How relevant is an evidence-based intervention's evidence to its real-world counterpart? Could the adapted or reinvented intervention even be called an evidence-based intervention? Or, if evidence-based interventions require adaptation and reinvention for real-world applicability, what are the real purposes or benefits of evidence-based interventions? Given such questions, we need to ask: Is the top-down approach the only path for ensuring scientific quality of health promotion/social betterment programs?

An Evidence-Based Intervention Does Not Necessarily Imply the Intervention Would Likely Be Real-World Effective

Even if an evidence-based intervention is implemented with high fidelity, it still does not necessarily imply the intervention would likely be real-world effective. Because of heavy emphasis on internal validity, evaluations following the top-down evaluation approach tend to neglect external validity. Usually, efficacy evaluations do not follow effectiveness evaluations (Green & Glasgow, 2006). In other words, evidence-based interventions in their current form usually provide little evidence of real-world generalizability. When advocates promote or disseminate to stakeholders an evidence-based intervention, those advocates must assume that the evidence-based intervention would likely be effective in the real world. The truth of this assumption is unknown because of a lack of effectiveness evaluations.

In fact, the small number of sequential evaluations that have been conducted has shown mixed results. On the one hand, interventions such as Coordinated Approach to Child Health (Luepker et al., 1996) have proven successful in research and real-world settings. On the other hand, the evaluation results of Reconnecting Youth (Hallfors et al., 2006) sounded real-world alarm bells. According to the initial efficacy evaluation of this program (Eggert, Thompson, Herting, Nicholas, & Dicker, 1994), among other things the intervention was found to decrease drug control problems and hard drug use and increase grade point average. But in a subsequent effectiveness evaluation, the intervention in a real-world setting showed not only that the program lacked desirable effects on drug control problems and school performance. On peer bonding, high-risk peer bonding, and socially desirable weekend activities, program adolescents actually had worse outcomes than did those in the control group (Hallfors et al., 2006). The authors argued that the harmful effects might have resulted from iatrogenic effects of grouping high-risk youth in a real-world setting.

Dissemination of evidence-based interventions is potentially precarious if that intervention's real-world transferability is unknown. As demonstrated in the Connecting Youth study, an evidence-based intervention might not only be ineffective in the real world, but it might even be harmful.

New Directions for Evaluation • DOI: 10.1002/ev

The Integrative Validity Model as an Alternative Typology to Address Validity Issues

The above case histories indicate that fundamental assumptions underlying the top-down approach do not always fit well with health promotion/social betterment program evaluation. And the problem cannot be easily resolved by technical strategies such as capacity building, technical assistance, or translational research. To address validity issues, program evaluation may need a more comprehensive perspective. This chapter proposes such a perspective, which we call the *integrative validity model*. Its premise is that any useful evaluation has to address both goal attainment and system integration issues (Chen, 1990, 2005, 2010). Goal attainment refers to whether an intervention can achieve the targets set for it. Goal attainment is important to stakeholders, but they are equally or even more interested in system integration. System integration means the extent to which an intervention can solve a problem by putting that intervention to work in a real-world system such as an organization or community. An intervention integrated into a system means the intervention is compatible or in synergy with other system components, such as missions, culture, manpower, structure, and capacity. The top-down approach is very strong in dealing with goal attainment issues, but often incapable of addressing system integration issues.

Note also that although goal attainment and system integration are related outcomes attributable to an intervention, they do not necessarily go hand-in-hand. An efficacious or effective intervention does not mean it integrates well with a community-based organization or vice versa. For example, a school-based intervention found to be efficacious may have problems in system integration if its implementation requires schools to overhaul their existing schedules. On the other hand, an intervention integrated well with a community-based organization does not necessarily mean the intervention is effective. DARE is a popular substance-abuse prevention program among schools, but evaluations have shown its ineffectiveness (Lynam et al., 1999). A successful intervention program means the program does well in both goal attainment and system integration.

To address goal attainment and system integration issues, the bottom-up evaluation perspective combines an integrative validity model and a bottom-up approach. The integrative validity model consists of three validity types: effectual, viable, and transferable (Chen, 2010). The model is a revision and expansion of Campbell and Stanley's distinction of internal and external validity (Campbell & Stanley, 1963) for evaluation purposes. In the model, *effectual validity* refers to the extent to which an evaluation provides evidence that an intervention causally affects specified outcomes. The concept is similar to interval validity. Effectual validity addresses issues of goal attainment.

To address system integration issues, the integrative validity model proposes a new concept of *viable validity*. Viable validity is the extent to which an intervention is viable in the real world. Here, viable validity refers to stakeholders' views and experience regarding whether an intervention program is real-world practical, affordable, suitable, evaluable, and helpful. More specifically, viable validity refers to whether ordinary practitioners—rather than research staff—can implement an intervention program adequately, and whether the intervention program is suitable for coordination or management by a service delivery organization such as a community clinic or a community-based organization. Additional questions are as follows:

1. Is the intervention program affordable?
2. Can it recruit ordinary clients without paying them to participate?
3. Does the intervention have a clear rationale for its structure and linkages connecting an intervention to expected outcomes?
4. Do ordinary clients and other stakeholders regard the intervention as helpful in alleviating clients' problems or in enhancing their well-being?

In this context, *helpful* is defined as whether stakeholders notice or experience progress in alleviating or resolving a problem.

As in other types of validity, viable validity takes into account threats to its integrity. For example, a threat of partiality means viewpoints of a major stakeholder group such as implementers or clients are neglected in evaluation. Partiality may cause evaluators to reach an improper conclusion on the viability of an intervention program. Fear of evaluation consequences means that stakeholders might be unwilling to provide candid information on viability because a negative result might damage the future of the program. Strategies for dealing with such threats include bringing in representatives from major stakeholder groups to plan the evaluation, triangulation of qualitative and qualitative data, an effective communication between evaluators and stakeholders on the purpose of the evaluation and use of evaluation data, or a combination thereof.

In the real world, stakeholders organize and implement an intervention program for the purpose of serving clients. Thus stakeholders have real viability concerns. The Resolving Conflict Creatively Program (RCCP) illustrates stakeholder interest in intervention viability. RCCP was a comprehensive, K–12 school violence-prevention program. School administrators liked the program because they considered it viable—in other words, they believed it worked. The program had been widely applied by many schools in several states for several years and then it was formally assessed by an effectiveness evaluation (Aber, Brown, Chaudry, Jones, & Samples, 1996).

The third type of validity in the integrative validity model is *transferable validity*. Transferable validity refers to the ability of intervention effectiveness or viability to transfer from research to real-world settings or from one real-world setting to another. The concept is different from the concept of external validity. Under the Campbell and Stanley validity typology (Campbell & Stanley, 1963), external validity asks the following question: "To what populations, settings, treatment variables, and measurement variables can this effect be generalized?" According to the definition, external validity is an endless quest for confirmation of an intervention's universal worth. This open-ended quest for generalizability may be appropriate for research, but it is impossible for evaluation to address generalizability issues adequately. The concept of transferable validity is developed for evaluation purposes. The definition of transferable validity has a boundary for transferability—the real world. Evaluators are capable of addressing transferability issues within the boundary. Furthermore, transferable validity expands the scope of external validity from effectuality to focus on both effectuality and viability to reflect stakeholders' interests better. Evaluators can use qualitative and/or quantitative methods to address transferable validity (Chen, 1990, 2005, 2010).

The integrative validity model also contributes to identifying viability evaluation—a new evaluation type that can assess the extent to which an intervention program is viable in the real world. Viability evaluation requires mixed (qualitative and quantitative) methods. On the one hand, evaluation relies on quantitative methods to collect data with which it can monitor progress on recruitment, retention, and outcome. On the other hand, evaluation requires an in-depth understanding of stakeholders' views and their experience with the specific intervention program.

The Bottom-Up Approach for Evaluating Health Promotion/Social Betterment Programs

The top-down approach has strengths in maximizing effectual validity or internal validity. However, to address comprehensively issues on viable, effectual, and transferable validity, we propose a bottom-up approach to program evaluation. The bottom-up approach provides a sequential route for strengthening validity in the reverse order of the top-down approach (Chen, 2010). To enhance viable validity (i.e., whether the intervention is practical, affordable, suitable, evaluable, and helpful), the evaluation sequence begins with a viability evaluation. If this real-world intervention is in fact viable, a subsequent effectiveness evaluation provides sufficient objective evidence of the intervention's effectiveness at the stakeholder, real-world level. If necessary for providing stronger evidence on transferability, additional effectiveness evaluations could also be conducted to address issues of whether such effectiveness and viability in this real-world setting is transferable to other real-world settings. First, evaluators need to deem the intervention viable, effective, and transferable in real-world evaluations. Then, if necessary, an efficacy evaluation using methods such as RCTs will rigorously assess a causal relationship between intervention and outcome and provide the strongest evidence on the intervention's efficacy.

New Directions for Evaluation • DOI: 10.1002/ev

Figure 8.1. Top-Down Approach vs. Bottom-Up Approach

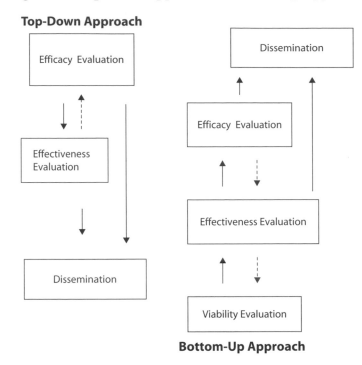

Differences between the top-down and bottom-up approaches are illustrated in Figure 8.1.

The bottom-up approach is particularly useful for evaluating health promotion/social betterment programs. A program usually starts as a real-world response to a pressing problem. The literature might provide some guidance. But stakeholders themselves are usually responsible for developing or putting the program together, and while doing so they usually face time and monetary constraints. Given such conditions, stakeholders often ask that an evaluation provide field evidence regarding whether the intervention (a) successfully reached and recruited participants, (b) had broad support from the community, (c) was smoothly run by an organization, and (d) allowed clients or other key stakeholders to feel that the intervention was helpful. Such information is useful to stakeholders for strengthening the same program in the future or for designing and implementing similar programs in other regions.

When stakeholders demand evidence of program viability, an initial viability evaluation is an appropriate methodology. Conducting a viability evaluation first to address viable validity issues makes sense, especially to demonstrate whether the program is practical and helpful in the real world. It does not mean, however, that stakeholders are uninterested in whether a causal relationship connects the intervention and the outcomes. Rather, they may feel that a lengthy and resource-intense efficacy evaluation does not fit their immediate evaluation needs; such an evaluation can wait until a future evaluation round.

Furthermore, instead of doing sequential evaluations, evaluators may be asked to conduct a single evaluation and deal with multiple validity issues. In conducting such a concurrent evaluation, evaluators face a challenging question: what type of evaluation is preferable for addressing validity issues? The bottom-up approach (Chen, 2010) suggests that evaluators must work with stakeholders to prioritize evaluation purposes, examine the nature of program stage and available resource, and select one of the following concurrent approaches for best serving stakeholders' needs: maximizing effectual validity, maximizing viable validity, or optimizing two or three types of validity.

The Usefulness of the New Perspective for Program Evaluation

The advantages of the new bottom-up perspective for program evaluation include the following.

Assure Intervention's Usefulness to Stakeholders and Avoid Wasting Money

The traditional top-down approach usually begins with an expensive and time-consuming efficacy evaluation to assess an innovative intervention. After millions of dollars are spent in an efficacy evaluation, it might be found that the efficacious intervention is very difficult to implement in the real world, not of interest to stakeholders, or may not be real-world effective. As a consequence, the evidence-based intervention may not be useful. This kind of approach tends to waste money and resources.

By contrast, the bottom-up approach starts from viability evaluation. This first assesses the viability of an intervention as proposed by researchers or stakeholders. The use of viability evaluation assures that an intervention has a good chance to survive in the real world before undertaking an expensive effectiveness or efficacy evaluation or both. Because interventions with low viability are screened out in the beginning, this approach could save funding agencies considerable money and resources. The bottom-up approach encourages funding agencies to fund many viability evaluations in communities to accumulate scientific knowledge on viable interventions and to select highly viable interventions for further rigorous studies.

Provide an Opportunity to Revise and Improve an Intervention in the Real World Before Its Finalization

One top-down approach limitation is finalizing the intervention protocol or package before or during efficacy evaluation—the protocol is not supposed to change after the evaluation. And when an intervention protocol is finalized at such an early stage, it prevents the intervention from gaining feedback from the real-world implementation or stakeholders' inputs for improvement. This approach seriously restricts an intervention's generalizability to the real world.

By contrast, the bottom-up approach affords an opportunity to improve an intervention during the viability evaluation. One viability evaluation purpose is to enhance the quality and usefulness of an intervention from organizational and community dynamics standpoints. Intervention protocols developed from stakeholder inputs and implementation experience increase their real-world relevancy and contribution.

Provide a Balanced View on Credible Evidence

Verifiable validity subsumes credible evidence from three components: viability, effectuality, and transferability. Under this perspective, evidence on intervention effectuality (internal validity) is not a stand-alone or context-free concept. Rather, it should be viewed or discussed with reference to viability and transferability. This perspective may aid those advocates of evidence-based intervention to move from currently narrow views of single-dimension evidence (effectuality) to a more balanced, multidimensional evidence model (viability, effectuality, and transferability).

Provide a Fresh Contingency View on Methods

As discussed in Chapter 1 of the issue, evaluators have debated intensely whether RCTs or other methods are the best evaluation methods. This new perspective provides a contingency view that may be useful in reconciling differences between the opposing camps. The contingency view argues different methods are useful for addressing different validity issues. For example, the view recognizes the power of RCTs in enhancing effectual validity or internal validity, but unlike the top-down approach, argues against a wide application of RCTs in evaluation. Instead, RCTs must be applied carefully and only for those interventions already assessed by viability evaluation and by effectiveness evaluation to avoid wasting money and other valuable resources.

Similarly, in addressing viable and transferable validity issues and advocating for their greater application in evaluation, the contingency view recognizes the essential value of qualitative methods. Unless effectual validity is conceptualized differently, qualitative methods alone are regarded generally as less powerful than are RCTs in ruling out effectual validity threats. Because the contingency view emphasizes strengths and limitations of different methods under different evaluation contexts, this view might be more acceptable to quantitative and qualitative camps and might be useful to reconcile differences between these two camps by narrowing differences or identifying common ground.

New Directions for Evaluation • DOI: 10.1002/ev

References

Aber, J. L., Brown, J. L., Chaudry, N., Jones, S. M., & Samples, F. (1996). The evaluation of the Resolving Conflict Creatively Program: An overview. *American Journal of Preventive Medicine, 12*(5 Suppl.), 82–90.

Bruzzese, J. M., Markman, L. B., Appel, D., & Webber, M. (2001). An evaluation of Open Airways for Schools: Using college students as instructors. *Journal of Asthma, 38*(4), 337–342.

Campbell, D. T., & Stanley, J. (1963). *Experimental and quasi-experimental designs for research.* Chicago: Rand McNally.

Chen, H. T. (1990). *Theory-driven evaluations.* Thousand Oaks, CA: Sage.

Chen, H. T. (2005). *Practical program evaluation: Assessing and improving planning, implementation, and effectiveness.* Thousand Oaks, CA: Sage.

Chen, H. T. (2010). The bottom-up approach to integrative validity: A new perspective for program evaluation. *Evaluation and Program Planning, 33*(3), 205–214.

Cook, T. D., & Campbell, D. T. (1979). *Quasi-experimentation: Design and analysis issues for field settings.* Chicago: Rand McNally.

Eggert, L. L., Thompson, E. A., Herting, J. R., Nicholas, L. J., & Dicker, B. G. (1994). Preventing adolescent drug abuse and high school dropout through an intensive school-based social network development program. *American Journal of Health Promotion, 8*(3), 202–215.

Evans, D., Clark, N. M., & Feldman, C. H. (1987). School health education programs for asthma. *Clinical Reviews in Allergy, 5*(3), 207–212.

Evans, R., 3rd, Gergen, P. J., Mitchell, H., Kattan, M., Kercsmar, C., Crain, E., et al. (1999). A randomized clinical trial to reduce asthma morbidity among inner-city children: Results of the National Cooperative Inner-City Asthma Study. *Journal of Pediatrics, 135*(3), 332–338.

Flay, B. R., Biglan, A., Boruch, R. F., Castro, F. G., Gottfredson, D., Kellam, S., et al. (2005). Standards of evidence: Criteria for efficacy, effectiveness and dissemination. *Prevention Science, 6*(3), 151–175.

Food and Drug Administration. (1992). *Guideline for the clinical evaluation of analgesic drugs.* Rockville, MD: Food & Drug Administration.

Green, L. W., & Glasgow, R. E. (2006). Evaluating the relevance, generalization, and applicability of research. Issues in external validation and translation methodology. *Evaluation & the Health Professions, 29*(1), 126–153.

Hallfors, D., Cho, H., Sanchez, V., Khatapoush, S., Kim, H. M., & Bauer, D. (2006). Efficacy vs effectiveness trial results of an indicated "model" substance abuse program: Implications for public health. *American Journal of Public Health, 96*(12), 2254–2259.

Joint Committee on Standards for Educational Evaluation. (1994). *The program evaluation standards* (2nd ed.). Thousand Oaks, CA: Sage.

Kattan, M. (2006). Moving research into the community: Learning by experience. *Annals of Allergy, Asthma & Immunology, 97*(1 Suppl. 1), S2–S3.

Luepker, R. V., Perry, C. L., McKinlay, S. M., Nader, P. R., Parcel, G. S., Stone, E. J., et al. (1996). Outcomes of a field trial to improve children's dietary patterns and physical activity. The Child and Adolescent Trial for Cardiovascular Health. CATCH collaborative group. *Journal of the American Medical Association, 275*(10), 768–776.

Lynam, D. R., Milich, R., Zimmerman, R., Novak, S. P., Logan, T. K., Martin, C., et al. (1999). Project DARE: No effects at 10-year follow-up. *Journal of Consulting Clinical Psychology, 67*(4), 590–593.

Rossi, P. H., Lipsey, M. W., & Freeman, H. E. (2004). *Evaluation: A systematic approach.* Thousand Oaks, CA: Sage.

Shadish, W. R., Cook, T. D., & Campbell, D. T. (2002). *Experimental and quasi-experimental designs for generalized causal inference.* Boston: Houghton Mifflin.

Veniegas, R. C., Kao, U. H., & Rosales, R. (2009). Adapting HIV prevention evidence-based interventions in practice settings: An interview study. *Implementation Science, 4*, 76.

Wandersman, A., Duffy, J., Flaspohler, P., Noonan, R., Lubell, K., Stillman, L., et al. (2008). Bridging the gap between prevention research and practice: the interactive systems framework for dissemination and implementation. *American Journal of Community Psychology, 41*(3–4), 171–181.

Williams, S. G., & Redd, S. C. (2006). From research to reality: From the National Cooperative Inner-City Asthma Study to the inner-city asthma implementation. *Annals of Allergy, Asthma, & Immunology, 97*(1 Suppl. 1), S4–5.

Huey T. Chen is a senior evaluation scientist of the Air Pollution and Respiratory Health Branch at the Centers for Disease Control and Prevention (CDC).

Paul Garbe is branch chief of the Air Pollution and Respiratory Health Branch at the Centers for Disease Control and Prevention (CDC).

Shadish, W. R. (2011). The truth about validity. In H. T. Chen, S. I. Donaldson, & M. M. Mark (Eds.), *Advancing validity in outcome evaluation: Theory and practice. New Directions for Evaluation, 130,* 107–117.

9

The Truth About Validity

William R. Shadish

Abstract

The chapters in Advancing Validity in Outcome Evaluation: Theory and Practice, *like the literature on validity in general, are extremely diverse. They range from a narrow focus on particular criticisms of validity in one recent work in the Campbell tradition to very broad overviews of methods for improving the generalizability of evaluation results. The author reviews and comments on each chapter, and discusses some general themes prompted by this issue of* New Directions for Evaluation. *Those themes include the ambivalent treatment of randomized experiments within the American Evaluation Association (AEA), the need for fresh ideas about outcome evaluations from outside the AEA community, and the desirability of an empirical program of evaluation theory in which data play a central role in our validity recommendations.* © Wiley Periodicals, Inc., and the American Evaluation Association.

I hope that the reader will forgive the cheekiness of the title of this commentary. It is meant to be at once provocative and challenging, self-deprecating and tongue-in-cheek (do I really think I have access to "the truth"?), yet also referential to the epistemological and ontological stances I find most congenial in their weak form. What I am really doing, of course, is speaking from my own little corner of the validity universe.

There is much to like in the chapters in *Advancing Validity in Outcome Evaluation: Theory and Practice*. They tackle ambitious and diverse intellectual agendas on an important contemporary question to the field of evaluation, validity in outcome evaluation. Yet that very diversity makes it difficult to write a coherent commentary. Indeed, a thoughtful review of just one of these chapters could be a chapter in itself. Given that limitation, I will first begin with observations about each of the chapters seriatim, and then try to draw together some resulting general thoughts.

Chen, Donaldson, and Mark

These authors set the stage for the issue by defining the theme and briefly reviewing the chapters (Chen, Donaldson & Mark, this issue). They note how this issue evolved from an initial focus on Donald Campbell's validity typology to its final and far more general focus on validity in outcome evaluation theory and practice. Some chapters still focus entirely on Campbell's validity typology, others make only passing reference to Campbell but do talk about validity, and still others talk about other features of good outcome evaluation but try to fit them into validity. The latter, in particular, raises a question. Validity may be essential to good outcome evaluation, but it is not clear that everything essential to good outcome evaluation needs to be placed into a validity typology. Imagine, for example, that this issue had evolved so that the theme was not validity but good outcome evaluation. Who could argue against, for example, the proposition that good outcome evaluation ought to consider not only accuracy but also utility, propriety, and feasibility? Or against the Chen and Garbe system integration issues? But are all these issues the province of validity? I think not, for then validity just becomes a catchall phrase for good, and we evaluators should know better than anyone that the good and the true are two different things.

Chen et al. also introduce an issue that is itself minor in some respects but that subsequent authors (e.g., Julnes, this issue; Mark, this issue; Reichardt, this issue) repeat and discuss, that the distinction between construct and external validity has been lost in recent works in the Campbell tradition. The issue pertains to an alleged change in the definition of construct and external validity from Cook and Campbell (1979; henceforth CC) to Shadish, Cook, and Campbell (2002; henceforth, SCC). It is not, from my perspective, true that the definition has changed. The prompt for this allegation seems to lie in the fact that CC mostly limited their discussion of construct validity to treatments and outcomes, whereas SCC provide more extended discussion of construct validity of persons and settings as well, and CC mostly limited their discussion of external validity to persons and settings, whereas SCC provide more extended discussion of external validity of treatments and outcomes, as well.

This expansion of application does not mean the definition has changed, in two respects. First, both CC and SCC use nearly identical language to define the fundamental idea of construct validity. SCC defines it as the "validity of inferences about the higher order constructs that represent sampling particulars" (p. 38); and CC defines it as the "validity with which we can make generalizations about higher-order constructs from research operations" (p. 38). Both references to higher-order constructs representing sampling particulars capture the essence of the original meaning of construct validity in Cronbach and Meehl (1955). That original meaning did not limit construct validity to treatments and outcomes, no surprise given that Cronbach and Meehl were writing in the context of test theory.

Second, given that CC focused more on the construct validity of treatments and outcomes, readers often overlook that they also said "construct validity concerns are not limited to cause and effect constructs. All aspects of the research require naming samples in generalizable terms, including samples of people and settings" (p. 59). The latter suggests that CC's choice to give only passing note to the construct validity of people and settings is not a denial of the intellectual merits of its inclusion. The more complete and systematic inclusion of people and settings in construct validity in SCC was motivated by formalizing and systematizing what was already present in CC. It is not new, and it is not a changed definition.

Gargani and Donaldson

The authors Gargani and Donaldson rightly point to the need for more attention to external validity broadly construed. Their advice about factors that increase the use of evaluations is sensible, especially their specific recommendations for involving stakeholders in use—though it would have been useful to contrast how those recommendations differ in important ways from the kinds of recommendations that have been salient in the evaluation utilization literature for decades.

Gargani and Donaldson (this issue) suggest " . . . the discussion of validity as it relates to outcome evaluation seems to be focused largely on questions of internal validity (Did it work?) with less emphasis on external validity (will it work?)" (p. 17). They provide no empirical evidence that this is the case. My impression is just the opposite. Outside the evaluation literature, for example, consider the medical literature on evidence-based practice. We know so much about how to assess what works that matters related to internal validity receive very little attention. By contrast, discussion of how such research translates into clinical practice is rampant. For instance, I subscribe to a list serve that sends me an average of about 10 journal articles per week about evidence-based practice. The October 11–15, 2010 article alert referenced 29 such articles, virtually all of which were reasonably construed as external validity (see http://www.citeulike.org/user/ SRCMethodsLibrary). Even within the confines of the American Evaluation Association (AEA), I would venture the guess that a review of *American Journal of Evaluation, New Directions for Evaluation*, or the program for AEA's annual conference would find more discussion of external validity than internal validity.

It is, however, interesting to note that the work of authors like Campbell (e.g., Campbell & Stanley, 1963), Cook (e.g., Cook and Campbell, 1979), and Rubin (e.g., Rubin, 1974) on descriptive causal inference is wildly popular and highly cited, whereas those same authors' work on things related to external validity (e.g., Cook's five principles of causal generalization, and Rubin's advocacy of response surface modeling in meta-analysis) remains nearly entirely unused and unreferenced by practicing evaluators. Why is that? I think it is because evaluators who are designing an evaluation are intuitively aware of the contextual embeddedness of their work, and of the virtual impossibility of anticipating future uses beyond those specified by the stakeholders to the evaluand. In that sense, Gargani and Donaldson are right to place the responsibility of use on stakeholders.

Mark

Mark's (this issue) chapter is also concerned with generalizability, and he provides a thoughtful set of recommendations for future practice and development on that topic. Mark focuses more than Gargani and Donaldson on things the evaluator can do to foster generalizability. They are excellent recommendations in principle, although they do vary in cost and feasibility. More important, they are premised on the claim that funders would not "allocate resources to evaluation if they assumed that it was a purely historical exercise with no generalizability to the times, clients, and setting(s) in which they are interested" (p. 31). This assumption is worth exploring for its validity. It seems just as plausible to say the opposite, that many funders of evaluation (as opposed to funders of research) are interested exactly in getting accountability data for a particular intervention. This might especially be the case for evaluators in AEA, more of whom probably do small-scale local evaluations than the kinds of large-scale randomized trials of potential policies more characteristic of the federal level. This suggests the need for more work on when it is and is not the evaluator's responsibility to attend more to external validity.

Mark alludes to this in his suggestion about doing research on stakeholder beliefs about generalizability. Calls for such research are frequent, but rarely done. Too much debate in evaluation theory, including most of the present volume, is uninformed by anything much resembling systematic evidence. More than a decade ago, I made the same observation about methodological theory, with a special focus on the failure of the Campbellian tradition to investigate empirically its own theory of quasiexperimentation (Shadish, 2000). Today that situation is greatly improved, and we can make many more data-based recommendations about our design and analysis recommendations (Shadish & Cook, 2009). If evaluation theory is really going to advance debate, it must have a substantial evidentiary component that it currently lacks.

Reichardt

I encourage readers to use Reichardt's (this issue) proposed typology if they find it useful. However, as the reader might suspect, I do not agree with his analysis of SCC, and find that three of the four criticisms of it are incorrect, and the fourth is trivial. First is the claim that SCC made external and construct validity equivalent. The argument is wrong in many ways. It goes wrong at the start in its incorrect assertion that all construct validity claims in SCC must refer to a causal inference: "When a higher-order construct is to be used in a causal inference, there is simply no other way to determine which challenges to construct validity must be accepted and which may be denied." Of course there is another way: "We use a **pattern-matching** logic to decide whether a given instance sufficiently matches the prototypical features to warrant using the category label" (SCC, p. 67). This is the method used since construct validity was first discussed (e.g., Cronbach & Meehl, 1955). SCC did not invent it. Of course, there is nothing wrong with reference to a causal inference in a construct validity argument. But it is unlikely that every term in every sentence used by evaluators refers to a causal inference, even when the evaluation has such an inference as a key focus. Under what rationale would evaluators have license to err about constructs that do not involve causal inference? Are we exempt from debates about, say, what constitutes "being black in the U.S. today"? (CC, p. 62). Of course not.

Reichardt's second criticism of SCC is that some people use the term *external validity* differently from SCC, and that they may also use *external validity* to mean something different from generalization. The point is correct, but also inherent in the ordinary use of language. The logical positivists tried to eliminate such problems, and failed. I doubt Reichardt will succeed, either. He then concludes that SCC is flawed because "A complete typology of criticisms of inferences should include the criticism that an inference is too narrow and not just that it is invalid" (p. 48). No logical grounds for such a claim exist at all, at least no more so than for the claim that a complete typology of criticisms of inferences ought to include any of a myriad of other new validity types proposed in this issue and elsewhere. A moment's reflection after reading this issue should reveal to any reader that a complete typology of criticisms of inferences is probably impossible.

Third, he claims SCC conflates validity and precision, concluding that "it is impossible for SCC to address properly the issue of precision under the rubric of validity" (p. 49). But he does not actually point to any errors in discussions of matters like power or heterogeneity or other things that affect precision in SCC. It seems this is just a disagreement about which word should be used. Lacking any evidence of an actual mistake, it is difficult to give this criticism much credence.

Fourth, he claims SCC omits time. We did omit it from the list of study facets: persons, settings, treatments, and measurements. We did so after considerable discussion, influenced by Cronbach (1982), who also omitted time from his UTOS model. That model said that all studies consist of units, treatments, observations, and settings (the first letters of each of these four words combining to form UTOS). Cronbach did not include time in his model. He argued that time has two parts. One is historical time (e.g., the Middle Ages, the Great Depression, the 1960s), where he thought replication of time is impossible. The second is temporal variables associated with treatment (length of treatment in time), measurement (length of follow-up), persons (birthdate), and settings (age of infrastructure). He argued that historical time should be omitted from study facets because it is not accessible to the researcher in any feasible way, and that the other aspects of time could be incorporated well enough into the other four facets. We followed his lead, but the decision is clearly debatable (if trivial). However, the extensive examples using time in SCC belie Reichardt's criticism that we omit it or otherwise give it short shrift.

Julnes

Julnes (this issue) has constructed another alternative validity typology. As I said about Reichardt's, I encourage readers to use it if they find it useful. Julnes notes that the inferences we make tend to overlap and so are best represented by overlapping dimensions. No doubt exists that the inferences overlap; SCC (pp. 93–102) discussed several such relationships and priorities. In addition, threats to validity also overlap in ways not much discussed in SCC. For example, attrition is listed as a threat to internal validity. But because sample size drops, it can threaten power (statistical conclusion validity), may require changing how we describe who is and is not in the study (construct validity), and may raise questions about whether the intervention would have the same effect in those who dropped out (external validity). I doubt that any system can eliminate all these overlaps, so there is much to be said for Julnes' embrace of them. Yet some simplicity is clearly lost. His figures show the potential proliferation, with 32 different types of possible inferences compared to SCC's 4. How well such complexity can serve as a teaching device or guide to practice is unclear. But Julnes' system is certainly an interesting intellectual exercise, especially as an illustration of the possible overlaps and innovations that might lie stated or unstated in the simpler SCC system.

Julnes' system is much larger for a second reason: He wants to develop a system covering all "the types of valid inference important to the evaluation community," (p. 57), not just causal inference with experiments. (It is not clear why Julnes describes SCC as "a general framework applicable to all research and evaluation" (p. 56) when SCC is clearly limited to cause-probing research and is not a book on evaluation at all.) In that goal he has, perhaps inevitably, failed, given that he does not include even all the validity types introduced in other chapters in this issue, much less those that have been posited in the past, such as Kirkhart's multicultural validity. Perhaps he could do so with more time, though the added complexity might reduce its practical utility even more.

House

House's characterizations of the Campbell tradition in all its variants are accurate, and reflect a careful read of and respect for original texts. His suggestions for how a revised typology might discuss conflict of interest and deliberate bias are reasonable. However, House's chapter might inadvertently leave the reader with the impression that researchers interested in internal validity are not sufficiently concerned with such matters. To the contrary, if we judge from the references House cites, it was the medical researchers themselves who surfaced the problems, and those researchers are certainly interested in internal validity.

House is trying to ensure that evaluators who are not sensitive to conflict-of-interest problems become so. This is a worthy goal. However, although it is desirable to call attention to this problem and seek remedies, we should recall that the sociology, psychology, and political economy of the contexts within which evaluations occur are constantly evolving. Any system we put into place to identify or prevent conflicts of interest and deliberate bias is likely to be gamed by the players to their own social, political, or economic advantage over time. Further, Campbell would emphasize that individual researchers are inherently limited in their ability to identify their own biases. He would place responsibility on the community of stakeholders to find such conflicts, stakeholders whose motivations may range from altruistic to revenge. I suspect House would agree.

Greene

Greene's chapter describes her interpretive/constructivist perspective on outcome evaluation. It is unclear what parts of her chapter refer to Campbellian approaches to validity. Unlike House, Greene almost never relates her ideas to specific things that people in the Campbell tradition have actually said. Early on, for example, she makes the claim that "widely accepted conceptualizations of validity rest on the assumption of an objective, neutral evaluator." She attributes the claim to House, who does not actually say this in his chapter, so the claim remains unattributed. If this refers to Campbell and colleagues, the claim is very badly wrong in very many ways, as House points out in some of his quotes from Campbell. Sometimes she does directly reference the Campbellian tradition, but incorrectly. For example, she dismisses Campbell's self-identification as an epistemological relativist by claiming Campbell relied on a procedural approach to validation. If procedure is meant to refer to experimental design, then the claim is again just wrong. Campbell described an inherently social theory of knowledge construction whereby the relevant community was best placed to surface problems in inferences.

Real differences between Campbell and Greene no doubt exist. Some are not based in differences in theory or intellectual principles, but rather reflect how to distribute limited resources in practice. For example, the resources Campbell would devote to experiments would not be available to spend as much time in context and on relationships, even though Campbell would agree on the latter's value to knowledge construction. Other differences may reflect intellectual disagreements. Take Greene's "interpretive evaluators likely rely relatively more on persuasive communications than empirical data" (p. 86). Because the bulk of most evaluation reports are probably persuasive communications, no matter who writes them, the question might be how little empirical data Greene thinks is enough—if we could find a way to measure the use of empirical data—and whether there is a cost in terms of knowledge construction due to having too little data. Finally, Campbell would have far less faith than Greene in the ability of any individual evaluator, interpretivist or not, to know "his or her own sociocultural history, beliefs about the social world and about what constitutes warranted knowledge of it, theoretical preferences, and moral and political values" (p. 82). He would worry that the interpretive evaluator who relied on his or her ability to know all this would be likely to increase bias, not decrease it.

Chen and Garbe

Chen and Garbe (this issue) propose an integrative validity model and a bottom-up approach to outcome evaluation. The chapter includes loose reference to Campbell as the root of a top-down approach in evaluation, though such a characterization never appears in Campbell's work in any form resembling the one in this chapter. That being said, the sentiment behind Chen and Garbe is understandable. When a federal funding agency like the Institute of Education Sciences makes clear it wants evaluators to jump right into randomized experiments that can be read as overlooking much of the pre-experimental work without which randomized experiments are much the worse. The Chen and Garbe recommendations for such pre-experimental work are sensible, although like Gargani and Donaldson, it is not clear what is new here other than the term *viable validity*.

I do appreciate the authors' use of empirical examples of interventions like Coordinated Approach to Child Health, and Reconnecting Youth, to bring evidence to bear on their contentions. It puts flesh on the bones of Mark's call for empirical research on matters treated in this issue. But not enough flesh. It is far too easy to find single examples that support or refute a position. Sampling error alone will guarantee that two identically done randomized experiments powered at .80 will only agree on whether the effect is significant or nonsignificant 68% of the time. If we want compelling evidence about whether efficacious interventions are later supported in effectiveness studies, we need a lot more cases than just two. Similarly, implicit in the proposals of Chen and Garbe is that too many efficacy studies are undertaken with insufficient evidence of viability. We need data on whether this is really the case. My own experience with such studies is that they are frequently grounded in extensive prior research and practice and would meet at least some of what Chen and Garbe seem to want, though obviously this might vary across content areas or funders.

New Directions for Evaluation • DOI: 10.1002/ev

Discussion

Randomized Experiments in the American Evaluation Association

Most of the contributors to this volume (and I) have been active in AEA for its entire existence, often in leadership positions, and were also members of AEA's predecessor organizations, Evaluation Network (ENet) and Evaluation Research Society (ERS). All of us know something about the organizational tensions that are perhaps illustrated in this volume, tensions born in the very different cultures of ENet and ERS. The former had members who were more likely to be local practitioners, to prefer qualitative methods, and to do small-scale or local evaluations; the latter had members more likely to be associated with federal and state agencies, to use quantitative methods, to look favorably on randomized experiments, and to be involved with large-scale evaluations of matters involving national policy. Tensions flared badly during the qualitative–quantitative debates of the late 1980s. They simmered during the 1990s, always obvious to the observant eye in the tendency for sessions at AEA's annual conferences to be segregated by the same groupings present at its birth. They flared again in the last 10 years as a result of an emphasis on randomized experiments in federal evaluation policy, a flare igniting the pages of this issue.

Indeed, I imagine that this volume would never have occurred without that emphasis, and that Campbell is merely a lightning rod for discontent with those experiments. Julnes (this issue) says this most clearly: " . . . [R]ecent controversies, such as the debates over federal policies promoting random-assignment experimental designs . . . have led some to criticize the SCC framework" (p. 56). This would go a long way toward explaining the uneven level of seriousness with which the chapters investigate what the Campbellian tradition actually says. In my experience, much of AEA has been unfriendly to randomized experiments, and the resulting culture has led to a brain drain from AEA among those interested in rigorous experimental methods, leaving AEA competent in many things but not those methods. AEA cannot afford to lose that expertise given its importance in modern evaluation policy.

Where Are the New Ideas for Outcome Evaluation?

Outside of AEA, I am not sure that anyone is debating validity typologies for outcome evaluation (though debates about validity for testing and assessment are active in education; e.g., Lissitz, 2009). Rather, researchers from such diverse disciplines as medicine, public health, statistics, and economics are investing their energy in solving the practical problems associated with experimentation, in finding methods by which research about effective treatments can be used to improve practice, and in creating ways to ameliorate the trade-offs that might be present regarding internal and external validity. I increasingly find those literatures more useful to my work than the evaluation literature. AEA certainly produces new and useful ideas for evaluation in general. But when it comes to outcome evaluation specifically, I get the sense of having the same recycled debates I have heard for decades.

Less Talk, More Data

I enjoy a good theoretical debate as much as the next guy. But my comments on a number of the chapters called for empirical data that could be used to clarify the validity of assumptions (e.g., whether it is true that we attend more to internal than external validity) or that could provide tests of theoretical claims that are part of a theory. Some of the contributors to this volume also make that call. Such data are too often absent in the debate, where claims are treated as logically necessary or implicitly compelling instead of as testable hypotheses. The result is reminiscent of the state of Aristotelian theory prior to the scientific revolution where theory was the dogma that dictated what data were acceptable rather than data being used to correct errors in dogma. Of course, things are not that black and white, but we are far too much of the former side of the continuum with a near total absence of data to inform our evaluation theory. Gathering data on matters like those treated in this book is admittedly difficult, but probably easier than doing evaluations themselves. At least some pertinent data exist already (e.g., Christie, 2003). What I am suggesting requires a cognitive change in which we think of our own claims as testable, develop the interest in doing so, and constantly spot-check ourselves to see whether we are making a claim that could be tested.

Conclusion

Outcome evaluation is experiencing a very exciting time right now. We are beginning to understand the conditions under which various kinds of non-randomized experiments might approximate results from randomized experiments (Shadish, Clark, & Steiner, 2008; Shadish, Galindo, Steiner, Wong, & Cook, in press). New approaches to causation are appearing and being combined with older ones (e.g., Shadish & Sullivan, in press). I wish I knew how to bring that sense of excitement and optimism about outcome evaluation into AEA.

References

Campbell, D. T., & Stanley, J. C. (1963). *Experimental and quasi-experimental designs for research*. Chicago: Rand-McNally.

Christie, C. A. (2003). What guides evaluation? A study of how evaluation practice maps onto evaluation theory. *New Directions for Evaluation, 97,* 7–36.

Cook, T. D., & Campbell, D. T. (1979). *Quasi-experimentation: Design and analysis issues for field settings*. Chicago: Rand-McNally.

Cronbach, L. J. (1982). *Designing evaluations of educational and social programs.* San Francisco: Jossey–Bass.

Cronbach, L. J., & Meehl, P. E. (1955). Construct validity in psychological tests. *Psychological Bulletin, 52,* 281–302.

Lissitz, R. W. (Ed.). (2009). *The concept of validity: Revisions, new directions and applications.* Charlotte, NC: Information Age Publishing.

Rubin, D. B. (1974). Estimating causal effects of treatments in randomized and nonrandomized studies. *Journal of Educational Psychology, 66,* 688–701.

Shadish, W. R. (2000). The empirical program of quasi-experimentation. In L. Bickman (Ed.), *Validity and social experimentation: Donald Campbell's legacy* (pp. 13–35). Thousand Oaks, CA: Sage.

Shadish, W. R., Clark, M. H., & Steiner, P. M. (2008). Can nonrandomized experiments yield accurate answers? A randomized experiment comparing random to nonrandom assignment. *Journal of the American Statistical Association, 103,* 1334–1343.

Shadish, W. R., & Cook, T. D. (2009). The renaissance of field experimentation in evaluating interventions. *Annual Review of Psychology, 60,* 607–629.

Shadish, W. R., Cook, T. D., & Campbell, D. T. (2002). *Experimental and quasi-experimental designs for generalized causal inference.* Boston: Houghton-Mifflin.

Shadish, W. R., Galindo, R. G., Steiner, P. M., Wong, V. C., & Cook, T. D. (in press). A randomized experiment comparing random to cutoff-based assignment. *Psychological Methods.*

Shadish, W. R., & Sullivan, K. (in press). Theories of causation in psychological science. In H. Cooper (Ed.), *APA handbook of research methods in psychology.*

WILLIAM R. SHADISH is a professor of psychology at the University of California, Merced.

INDEX

NEW DIRECTIONS FOR EVALUATION

ORDER FORM SUBSCRIPTION AND SINGLE ISSUES

DISCOUNTED BACK ISSUES:

Use this form to receive 20% off all back issues of *New Directions for Evaluation*.
All single issues priced at **$23.20** (normally $29.00)

TITLE	ISSUE NO.	ISBN

*Call 888-378-2537 or see mailing instructions below. When calling, mention the promotional code JBNND
to receive your discount. For a complete list of issues, please visit www.josseybass.com/go/ev*

SUBSCRIPTIONS: (1 YEAR, 4 ISSUES)

☐ New Order   ☐ Renewal

U.S.	☐ Individual: $89	☐ Institutional: $271	
CANADA/MEXICO	☐ Individual: $89	☐ Institutional: $311	
ALL OTHERS	☐ Individual: $113	☐ Institutional: $345	

*Call 888 378-2537 or see mailing and pricing instructions below.
Online subscriptions are available at www.onlinelibrary.wiley.com*

ORDER TOTALS:

Issue / Subscription Amount: $ _____

Shipping Amount: $ _____
(for single issues only – subscription prices include shipping)

Total Amount: $ _____

SHIPPING CHARGES:	
First Item	$5.00
Each Add'l Item	$3.00

*(No sales tax for U.S. subscriptions. Canadian residents, add GST for subscription orders. Individual rate subscriptions must
be paid by personal check or credit card. Individual rate subscriptions may not be resold as library copies.)*

BILLING & SHIPPING INFORMATION:

☐ **PAYMENT ENCLOSED:** *(U.S. check or money order only. All payments must be in U.S. dollars.)*

☐ **CREDIT CARD:**   ☐ VISA   ☐ MC   ☐ AMEX

Card number _____ Exp. Date _____

Card Holder Name _____ Card Issue # _____

Signature _____ Day Phone _____

☐ **BILL ME:** *(U.S. institutional orders only. Purchase order required.)*

Purchase order # _____
Federal Tax ID 13559302 • GST 89102-8052

Name _____

Address _____

Phone _____ E-mail _____

Copy or detach page and send to: **John Wiley & Sons, PTSC, 5th Floor**
989 Market Street, San Francisco, CA 94103-1741

Order Form can also be faxed to: **888-481-2665**

PROMO JBNND